THE CAPE OF GOOD HOPE
A JOURNEY OF DISCOVERY

THE CAPE OF GOOD HOPE
A JOURNEY OF DISCOVERY

URSULA STEVENS

Wanderlust Books
A Division of Wanderlust Tours cc
Reg.No. CK 9771146423
P.O.Box 303 Paarden Eiland 7420 South Africa
E-mail: wanderlust@iafrica.com

First published 1999

ISBN 0-620-24899-8

PUBLISHER	Wanderlust
ILLUSTRATOR	Renate Stitfall
REPRODUCTION	Castle Graphics (Pty) Ltd
PRINTING	Paarl Printing (Pty) Ltd

CONTENTS

	PAGE
INTRODUCTION	7
TRAVELLERS ADVICE	8
From the City to Clifton	10
From Clifton to Hout Bay	21
From Hout Bay to Kommetjie	30
From Kommetjie to Cape Point	39
From Cape Point to Simon's Town	62
From Simon's Town to Groot Constantia	78
From Groot Constantia, via Kirstenbosch and Rhodes Memorial to the City	92
An Historical Outline to 1806	100
Other Stories Told	104
Brief Statistical Profile	108
Bibliography	109
Index	110

ACKNOWLEDGEMENTS

The Seeligers were amongst the first families to settle permanently in Kommetjie at the turn of the century. Over the years I have listened to the many wonderful stories told by the late Anni Seeliger about her childhood days in Kommetjie, stories of the sea, shipwrecks, people and events. I am very grateful to her. My thanks also go to Lionel Mundell for his editorial input and constructive criticism; to the many travellers I met and whose questions and curiosity helped to unlock the cultural and historical treasure trove of the Peninsula; and of course, to my husband who always makes the impossible possible for me.

INTRODUCTION

A colourful tapestry of diverse political,cultural and religious beliefs, distinct racial and societal characteristics has been woven together over the centuries. From the earliest inhabitants to seafarers and adventurers; from travellers of foreign shores to slaves and refugees from Africa and the East; from poets and writers to musicians: all have left their stamp on the Peninsula.

Cabo Tormentoso, The Cape of Storms, The Fairest Cape, The Cape of Good Hope - what best describes this magnificent expanse of land at the foot of Africa?

The natural attractions of the Peninsula are equally diverse: mountains, sea, fauna and flora compete with each other, indeed the Cape Peninsula's beauty is intoxicating.

It is the aim of this book to briefly sketch the Cape Peninsula's colourful history and to catapult you into the magic of the area, to discover for yourself the fascinating places and incomparable beauty.

TRAVELLERS' ADVICE

The early travellers fittingly described the Cape as the 'Cape of Storms'. Thus, whether you set off in summer or winter, be prepared for gentle breezes, strong or gale force winds. Even if for once the city bowl enjoys a windfree day, there is no telling what may await you at the Cape. Nobody has yet harnessed the moods of the wind!

On a sunny, warm day pack your bathing costume, sun hat and suntan lotion, as the beaches may tempt you. The roads can be severely congested over weekends, particularly middle to late afternoon along the False Bay coastline. The reason? Capetonians are returning from Cape Point picnic and fishing spots, or the beaches.

Close to Easter, a major cycle race with well over 25 000 participants leads to the temporary closure of some of the route. Check before setting out, whether your journey coincides with the cycle race.

Similarly, the Two Oceans Marathon takes places in March/April. The runners may well block your road, so please establish the date, should you travel during those months.

After heavy rains, establish whether or not 'Chapman's Peak Drive' is open to traffic. This scenic route can be closed by the authorities due to the possibility of rockfall in wet conditions.

For some it might be the first time that you are travelling on the left side of the road. Your understandable nervousness is probably going to be heightened by the fairly ill-disciplined local traffic users. Take care! Beware of vehicles turning off, stopping, overtaking (on either side of you) without signalling their intentions or decide to make a U-turn. Please do not give lifts to hitch-hikers. When you park your car, do not leave valuables inside. If possible, conceal any surplus bags in the boot.

Please do not throw cigarette ends out of the window. Fires destroy, and our mountains and animals will thank you for your concern.

Do not fear for your physical well-being as all along the route, restaurants and coffee shops beckon; unless, of course, you prefer to enjoy a picnic en route.

Make sure you have enough film rolls or video tapes! Although freely available you don't want to run out just when that magic view unfolds before your eyes.

Allow a whole day for the approximately 200 km long excursion.

Petrol is readily available; the last filling station before Cape Point is in Kommetjie, and the first one after leaving the Reserve in Simon's Town.

"NM" in text stands for National Monument.

And last, but not least, should baboons block your path, close your windows! They are dangerous and uncommonly resourceful at getting into cars - something you definitely want to avoid. Please do not feed them! Feeding a baboon is punishable by law.

FROM THE CITY TO CLIFTON

The route in outline:

Cape Town (City/Waterfront)- Mouille Point - Sea Point - Bantry Bay - Clifton - Camps Bay - Bakoven - Llandudno - Hout Bay - Chapman's Peak - Noordhoek - Kommetjie - Scarborough - Cape Point - Seaforth - Simon's town - Fish Hoek - Kalk Bay - Muizenberg - Groot Constantia - Kirstenbosch - Rhodes Memorial-Cape Town.

Starting point is in the city centre, in **Adderley Street**, near the Fountain and the Cape Town Railway Station.

The street name pays tribute to the British parliamentarian Charles B.Adderley. A staunch supporter of colonial self-government, he endeared himself to Capetonians in the middle of the 19th century when he vehemently opposed the extraordinary decision, to transform the Cape into a penal colony. A huge outcry met the British proposal. Capetonians, supported by the exhortations of Anti-Convict League speakers and Charles B.Adderley succeeded in their resistance and the 'Neptune' at anchor in Cape waters for nearly five months, left for Australia.

Conspicuous in the centre of the street is the **War Memorial**. It honours the city's soldiers who made the supreme sacrifice in the two World Wars and the Korean War. Looking down Adderley Street, towards the **Fountain**, the statue of the founder of the city, Jan van Riebeeck, created by the sculptor John Tweed can be seen, and next to him that of his wife, Maria de la Queillerie, crafted by the Dutch sculptor Dirk Wolbers.

Looking towards the mountain, the **'Golden Acre'** shopping complex with its underground malls comes into view. On this site ruins of the first water reservoir were discovered. Built under Governor Zacharias Wagenaar (1663 - 1666), it provided passing ships and townsfolk with fresh water. Built of Malmesbury shale and brick in the bed of the **'Fresh Water'** stream, known by the Dutch as the **'Verse River'** and by the Khoikhoi as the **'Camissa'**, it held 700 cubic metres of water. Four steps led up to the 1m-high wall enabling the sailors to scoop out buckets of water.

At the first set of traffic lights turn right into **VAN RIEBEECK STREET**.

This street, together with Strand Street, once formed the shoreline of Table Bay. The Dutch knew Table Bay as **'Roggebaai'** ('Bay of Skate'),a fish then plentiful in the bay. Here too the first locally built boat, the 'Brydegroom'

('Bridegroom') was launched in 1663. It transported shale from Robben Island to the main land, fish and seals from Saldanha or penguin eggs from Dassen Island, on the West Coast. Imagine the cosy little fishermen's cottages along the former shore, smells of fish drying in the sun, nets being mended and watercarts wheeled by. All these memories were deeply buried under the huge landfill when the area, stretching northeasterly towards the busy docks and measuring some 140 ha was reclaimed from the sea, necessitated by the construction of Duncan Dock, named after the first South African appointed Governor General, Sir Patrick Duncan. Construction work began before the Second World War. That area is now known as the 'Foreshore'.

Travel on and turn right into BUITENGRACHT STREET,('Outer Canal') once the westerly border of the old town, select the left lane, then turn left into WESTERN BOULEVARD, and at the next set of traffic lights, right into PORTSWOOD ROAD. (signposted: WATERFRONT/SOMERSET) At the IMAX/BMW CENTRE turn left into BEACH ROAD.

Beach Road runs along the periphery of the **V&A WATERFRONT**, an exciting commercial and leisure development around Cape Town's original harbour.

On the left, notice **SOMERSET HOSPITAL**, which dates back to 1862. Governor Sir George Grey laid the corner stone for this hospital which also trained the first medical students. It is named after Lord Charles Somerset, Governor of the Cape from 1814 to 1827.

Somerset Hospital

You also catch a glimpse of 'Fort Wyngard', site of the South African Coast Guard and Anti-Aircraft Artillery Museum.

The pleasant drive past the golf course and along the Atlantic shore leads through the suburb of **MOUILLE POINT**.

What does this strange name mean?

Sailors feared Table Bay, especially in winter when angry storms lashed the sea. To provide more sheltered anchorage, Governor Swellengrebel proposed to construct a breakwater in 1743. But where to find the money? The tight fisted Company could hardly be approached. Not lacking in imagination, the governor targeted the farmers for assistance: once they had delivered their goods in town, they had to reload their wagons with stones, drive out to Mouille Point and off-load them.

Wagon after wagon rumbled towards the shore dumping its cargo into the sea. This had a spin off effect as now the good citizens of Cape Town, the burghers, lent a helping hand. They freed their slaves temporarily from domestic duty to provide labour, whilst the authorities put convicts to work. Three long years they toiled, but in vain. Construction finally ceased. Whether it was a lack of funds or dwindling enthusiasm for the scheme, or the indomitable wild Atlantic Ocean, will never be known. Some 100m of a breakwater which the Dutch called a 'moilje' had been built.

In 1781 the French, as allies of the Dutch, arrived in the Cape. They erected a battery near the unfinished mole, naming it Mouille Point Battery.(The French 'mouiller' means 'dropping anchor'.)

Presently the **GREEN POINT LIGHTHOUSE**, clad in bright red and white stripes appears. Built by the German architect Hermann Schütte and commissioned in 1824, it is the oldest working lighthouse in the country. Countless lighthouse keepers were trained here. From a height of 20 metres, one flash every ten seconds alerts passing ships far out at sea, as it has a range of

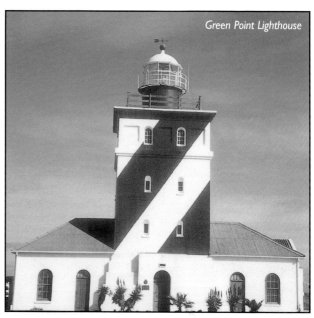

Green Point Lighthouse

25 sea miles (55,36 km). The light was electrified in 1929 and intensified to 850 0000 CD.

Nearby residents probably resent the Lighthouse, as during certain times of the year its nautophone foghorn disturbs their sleep.

Not far from the shore, looking across the Atlantic, **ROBBEN ISLAND**, is visible. This small island - it is about 2km wide and 3,5 km long - has endured a colourful, often painful history.
Once Dias and da Gama had established the sea route to the east, ships in ever increasing numbers broke the treacherous voyage at the Cape, replenishing dwindling supplies. Frequently they anchored near the island's shores known to English sailors as 'Penguin Island'. But it was the Dutch 'Robbe Island'('Sea-Dog Island') which endured.

In 1601, Sir James Lancaster, an English mariner, left behind a a truly generous gift of sheep! They were to become a constant meat supply for future fleets, thus releasing sailors from the sometimes perilous task to barter for meat on the mainland. His hopes were however, dashed. The next fleet, commanded by a Joris van Spilbergen slaughtered the entire flock. The idea, though, of guarding sheep on the island, lingered on and persisted once the Dutch East India Company had gained a foothold at the Cape with the arrival of Jan van Riebeeck in 1652.

The island was probably also the country's first post office, albeit unofficial. Anxious to receive and pass on news, sailors used to hide their letters and messages at designated spots.

The hill rising above the suburbs of Mouille Point and Green Point is the popular **SIGNAL HILL** (350m).

Daily, except on Sundays, the boom of the **Noon Gun** echoes through the city, a cloud of smoke rises in the mid-day sky, and Capetonians glance furtively at their watches, a time-honoured tradition!

During the First British Occupation in 1795, the Dutch guns were removed from Imhoff Battery at the Castle and replaced by about 25 English 18-pounder guns. Designed by Captain Thomas Blomefield and marked by serial numbers, these guns were cast between 1788 and 1779, bearing the monogram of King George III (1760-1820).

A CHRONOLOGICAL JOURNEY OF THE ISLAND

1488: Dias anchors in Table Bay on his return voyage.

1497 -1503: Visits to the island by Vasco da Gama and Antonio de Saldanha.

1525: A Portuguese ship reportedly leaves convicts behind.

1611: Dutch sailors shipwrecked.

1615: English convicts under John Cross seek refuge.

1632 -1640: Group of Khoikhoi settled voluntarily on the Island led by Autshumao, also known as Harry.

1647: The survivors of the Dutch ship 'Harlem' get penguin eggs from the Island.

1652: Van Riebeeck obtains eggs, penguin meat, train oil and shell-lime from island.

1655: System of signal fires and beacons established to assist shipping in Table Bay.

1673: Five imprisoned Khoikhoi succeed in escaping.

1682: First Indian exile, a prince from the Island of Macassar is sent to Island.

1742: Prince of Madura imprisoned.

1744: First Muslim holy men banished to Island.

1750: Daing Mangenam, Prince of Macassar, exiled.

1806 -1807: Prisoners on Island removed by the British because it is feared they will assist the French or Dutch in an attack on the Cape. British military convicts now sent to Island.

1819: Xhosa prophet from the eastern Cape, Makana, also known as Nxele or Links, imprisoned for his rôle in leading the Ndlambe Xhosa against the British in Frontier War of 1818/19.

1820: Makana masterminded a mass escape from the island, together with two white prisoners, Schmidt and Holmes. Makana's boat capsized and he drowned near Blouberg Strand.

1841: English church built by convicts.

1846: Lepers arrive, plus chronic sick from the Pauper Asylum (Old Slave Lodge) and the Old Somerset Hospital plus lunatics from the hospital.

1858: Ngqika Xhosa arrive as prisoners after the Cattle Killing on the Eastern Frontier in the Cape; they were released conditionally in 1866.

1866: More convicts brought to perform manual labour.

1891: Leprosy Repression Act passed. Number of lepers on Island increases and chronic sick are removed from Island.

1921: Last lunatics removed. Some convicts remain.

1931: All lepers transferred to other leper asylums.

1936: Island declared a military reserve by Minister of Defence O. Pirow.

1960: First political prisoners arrive and start building a high security prison. Naval base still on Island. Bans on Royal Cape yachts and fishermen coming too close or sheltering there in high seas.

1976: Activists after Soweto rising sent to Island.

1982: Many political prisoners removed to Pollsmoor, including Nelson Mandela.

1991: Last political prisoners removed.

1997: Island declared a National Monument.

By 1807 one of them was fired daily, at first in the morning and at sunset. The gun was fired in conjunction with the Time-Balls in the harbour.

Before 1864, a flare pistol fired from the roof of the Observatory, signalled the accurate time to the gunner. As soon as he had spotted the flare he would fire the gun. However, from 1864, the gun was fired by electrical detonators set off via an electrical signal from the Observatory.

In August 1902, two of the 18-pounder smooth bore muzzle loader guns bearing the serial numbers 17 and 54, were transported by ox wagon to Lion Battery on Signal Hill. They were eventually replaced by three 6-inch Mk XXIV mountings in March 1944.

The original time gun was one of the means by which ships in Table Bay could determine the error and rate of their chronometers, although in those early days the signals were given at one o'clock. The introduction of modern time signals on February 6, 1925 made time balls and the Noon Gun obsolete, but fortunately for Capetonians, the latter was retained: how else would they be able to tell the time?

During World War II the boom of the Noon Gun was the signal for a two minute pause in remembrance of the soldiers at the Front.

The news of victory in Europe was celebrated with a gun salute from Lion

Battery on May 8, 1945.

The city's saluting battery, which was mounted on the Katzenellenbogen Bastion at the Castle till 1939, was later also moved to Lion Battery. It now consists of four 12-pounder quick-firing guns which are manned by naval gunners on State occasions such as the Opening of Parliament and visits of foreign dignitaries.

Yet, Signal Hill is not indebted to the Noon Gun for its name.

In the days of the Company, signalmen were stationed in the *nek* formed by Table Mountain and Lion's Head,- then also known as 'Vlaggeman's Hoogte' or 'Flagman's Height', on Lion's Head, and on the 'Lion's Rump'. They scanned the horizons for any approaching fleet and alerted the Castle by raising and lowering a flag, thus signalling not only the approach of a fleet but also its size.

At the traffic lights immediately after the Green Point Lighthouse, turn right into Beach Road.

You are in **THREE ANCHOR BAY**.

Soon after van Riebeeck's landing, a handful of sailors ventured out and discovered a sandy inlet, naming it 'De Leeuwen Zandbaeikjen' - the 'Lion's Cove'. Years later, a small defense building was erected here, the 'Sailor's Fort' and finally, a defence chain, held up by three anchors so as to prevent any hostile landing was fixed across the bay, giving the suburb its name.

THE GEOLOGICAL CONTACT IN SEA POINT

During the Precambrian era about 600-800 million years ago sedimentary formations of the Malmesbury Group were deposited. Large parts of Cape Town are underlain by these sedimentary formations.

The strata along the Atlantic seafront were deeply buried and the sediments compacted and hardened into dark fine-grained rocks. Millions of years later, the sub-marine sedimentary basin was uplifted and a mountain chain created in which the deeper strata had been tightly folded.

Intense heat coming from the core of the earth then melted the crust of this mountain chain and granitic magma penetrated into the folded Malmesbury strata and solidified at great depth. This pluton underlies the Cape Peninsula.

The intruding granite forced aside pre-existing country rock or assimilated it. The fold structures in the Malmesbury strata guided intrusion, so that the contact between country rock and granite follows the strike of the steeply dipping beds at Sea Point.

Over a period of some 100 million years, the granite pluton deep in the mountain chain was uplifted, eroded and finally exposed about 500 million years ago in a plain-like region bordering on an ancient coastline.

On to this base the sediments of the Cape Supergroup were subsequently deposited. The sediments hardened and compacted into sandstone that are now exposed on the cliffs of Table Mountain, Devil's Peak and Lion's Head. The sandstone and shale layers had reached a depth of about 3000 metres, burying the old platform. But further enormous earth movements uplifted the old base above the present sea-level. Erosion along the present Atlantic coast forced the sandstone cliffs to retreat to their present locations, revealing the granite and its contact with the Malmesbury strata at Sea Point.

The road swings south-westerly and reaches **SEA POINT**.

Sea Point earned early fame in 1776, when part of Captain Cook's expedition to Australia encamped here. Today Sea Point is a densely populated suburb, known for its many good restaurants, good shopping facilities. Along the beach front the pleasant promenade invites the strollers, and the green lawns call the picnic-lovers.

Travelling on, Beach Road soon forks. Bear left. To the right you pass a low brick building, the **Sea Fisheries Research Aquarium**. Here scientists can simulate a variety of oceanic conditions - light, temperature and oxygen levels - and study their effects on marine resources. It is the only facility of its kind in the country and significantly contributes towards the relatively new science of mariculture (sea farming).

At the traffic circle allow for a small detour to witness a striking geological phenomenon. Swing right and turn towards the sea.

An information board explains the exposed contact zone between the dark shale of the Malmesbury Series and the intrusive lighter coloured Cape granite. This unusual circumstance, first noted by Clark Abel in 1818, fascinated Charles Darwin who visited this site in 1836. It is a National Monument.

*The brief geological excursion ends. Drive back towards the traffic circle and turn into Queens Road, straight towards the unmistakable silhouette of **LION'S HEAD**.*

Lions Head

The mountain has known many different names.

In 1620 Commodore FitzHerbert set foot on Cape soil, took possession of the land in the name of England and King James, and duly hoisted a flag on the hill he called 'Saint James Mount'.

Other sailors dubbed it 'Ye sugar Loafe', before the early Dutch settlers finally chose 'Leeuwenbergh' - 'The Lion Mountain'. The mystery remains whether feared encounters with lions or the mountain's resemblance to a crouching lion inspired the name? Van Riebeeck himself recorded in his journal(1652) that he had landed near the 'Lion's tail'. The last lion on the hills, it is said, was shot in the middle of the 19th century.

But for its true moment of glory Lion's Head had to wait till 1886, when the discovery of some gold quartz, on the Cape Town side of the mountain, ignited the big gold rush.

By May, gold fever had gripped the townsfolk's imagination. Hastily the 'Lion's Head (Cape Town) Gold Mining Company' was launched. Prospectors were digging frenetically, and fortune seekers everywhere scrambled up the slopes. Shafts were sunk into the mountain near Bantry Bay, Fresnaye but hélas, all to no avail. Samples sent to Europe revealed the sad truth: it lacked quality and the demise of the gold mining company was inevitable.

About 80 m up the road turn sharply right into Victoria Road (M 6). You have reached **BANTRY BAY**, *once known as 'BOTANY BAY'.*

In 1787, Dr Friedrich Ludwig Liesching from Stuttgart in Germany, settled in the Cape, on completion of his military service as a surgeon-major. In his native Germany he had been a friend of the distinguished German poet Friedrich von Schiller.

Driven by his life-long passion, botany, he and another ardent amateur botanist friend, Johann de Ziegler, dreamed of a botanical garden for the cultivation of medicinal herbs and other rare plants. They earmarked the lower slopes of Signal Hill: a spring would supply abundant water and it could comfortably be reached by wagon. The authorities though willing to grant the land, attached certain conditions. Thus, the spring's water supply would have to remain accessible to the public for the watering of cattle, the existing track to Camps Bay had to be kept open and the ground was to be developed for the exclusive use of a garden only.

Liesching and de Ziegler worked energetically, constructing terraces, transporting suitable soil to the site which ultimately extended from the mountain slopes to the great granite boulders on the water's edge. The garden became a show place. Distinguished visitors arrived, amongst others the Rev. C.I. Latrobe in 1816 and in 1817, the Marquis Emmanuel de las Casas, Napoleon's chamberlain who had accompanied the emperor to his island exile, St. Helena. Suspected of having smuggled messages, the Marquis and his young son were expelled from the island and sent to the Cape. After a brief stay here, de las Casas returned to France.

Today, Bantry Bay is a much sought after suburb of Cape Town - glance up the mountain slopes to appreciate the superb position enjoyed by many of the houses. Another reason for its popularity, so it is said, is the relative lack of the dreaded south-easterly winds, the famous 'Cape Doctor' which elsewhere can become the scourge of Capetonians.

THE CAPE DOCTOR - THE SOUTH-EASTERLY WIND

This wind, affectionately known as the 'Cape Doctor'. blows mainly during the summer months, making its first appearance during early spring in September, lasting through to the end of April. It is a trade wind, originating in the South Atlantic High pressure system. This systems moves further southwards in summer as the westerlies retreat polewards. It then ridges south of the country where it joins with the South Indian High pressure system, often forming a band of high pressure to the south of the country during summer. The speed varies from 20 to 125 km/h - at times even higher. During extreme south-easter conditions windspeeds double-decker buses have been blown over, and pedestrians whirled about.

EARLY BUSES, TRAMS TO SEA POINT

In 1861 the 'Cape Town and Green Point Tramway Company' was established to operate horse-trams between the city and Sea Point. The grand opening festivities on 30 April 1863 were sadly, overshadowed by a severe outbreak of influenza.

The tram left from Long Street, rumbling cheerfully towards Sea Point, the terminus. Some 25 passengers found seats in the 'Victoria', 'Albert', 'Empress' or the 'Queen', and late comers rode on top, braving the weather. On a platform in front of each car, a man clutching a pole was positioned whose specific job it was to push stones out of the way. But still, passengers were jolted about and conversation was difficult with all the rattling going on.

The service proved so popular that by 1879 twelve trams ran daily, in each direction. The last car left Cape Town at 17h15.

Thirty minutes before departure a bell alerted potential passengers who boarded or alighted anywhere along the route. Guards would jump off to deliver parcels along the road, and on certain nights, a special 'Drunks Tram' saw to the safe return of revellers!

The tramway boosted development in Sea Point as tram sheds, stables and a forge were set up, and cottages built for the drivers and labourers.

Eventually, the Green Point Tramway Company amalgamated with the City Tramways Company, forming the 'Metropolitan Tramways Company'. It operated the first electric trams in 1896 - the end of an era as the horse-trams disappeared from the scene.

The new electric double-deckers made life downstairs a little more bearable for the passengers. But on the upper deck, despite a roofed top, they still wrestled with the elements. Fierce winds and driving rains rushed in through the open sides which were only later glassed in. Perhaps the journey was faster, more efficient, but the trams were as noisy as their forerunners. Outside churches notices went up asking the 'tram cars to run dead slow on Sundays during the hours of divine service.'

About 1919 the first single-decker motor buses were put into service, running in conjunction with the trams.

In 1939 the trams were replaced by the now defunct trolley-buses.

FROM CLIFTON TO HOUT BAY

Shortly **CLIFTON** with its four sandy inlets, the popular Clifton beaches, is reached. The 'bungalows' perched on the water's edge were built during World War I as temporary homes, in a time of a housing shortage. Today they are much prized and sought after properties.

Clifton was also once known as 'Schoenmaakers Gat' ('Shoemaker's Hole') as a shoemaker had made his home here in a cave.

Continue along the splendid coastal road. Just before reaching CAMPS BAY, turn right into a large tarred parking area 'Maiden's Cove'. Looking down from the hill opposite is the Camps Bay High School. Take a few minutes to delight in the white sandy beach and the 'Twelve Apostles' towering over the bay.

Leaving 'Maiden's Cove', turn right for **CAMPS BAY**.

Camps Bay

For centuries the foothills of the Apostles had enticed people to settle here. Who could resist the dazzling views across the Atlantic? On this narrow coastal plain, Khoikhoi grazed their sheep long before van Riebeeck permitted the Goringhaiquas in 1657 to 'live behind the kloof between the Table and Lion mountains along the shore to the south west of the Fort'. Then the first Dutch farmers arrived and developed the land which was to become known as 'Ravensteyn'.

In 1778, the authorities allowed Fritz von Kamp, a sickly German sailor from Mecklenburg, to remain in the Cape. Fortune smiled on him when he met the wealthy widow Anna Wehrnich, owner of the Ravensteyn farm. The two wed and soon the bay was called 'Die Baay van von Kamptz', today's Camps Bay. Whilst the young couple was visiting Holland, war erupted in Europe, which put Holland at loggerheads with England. The Dutch authorities at the Cape feared an enemy attack and a possible landing at Camps Bay.

Defensive measures that were hastily undertaken included the building of a battery, trenches were dug and the road linking Camps Bay to Cape Town made impassable. When von Kamptz returned after the war, he found the farm lying in ruins. In 1788 it was sold to the Government.

Other well-known occupants of the farmhouse in the early part of the 19th century, were the English governors Lord Caledon and Lord Charles Somerset. The latter believed Camps Bay militarily to be at risk and added a guardhouse to the battery, enlarged the house and had the road repaired. The remains of the old battery stand below Kloof Road, to the left, near where Kloof Road joins the coastal road at the entrance to Camps Bay.

THE TWELVE APOSTLES

Camps Bay nestles at the foot of rock buttresses that the early settlers knew first as 'Gable Mountains', and later only as the 'Twelve Apostles'. Curious indeed, as a thorough count of the buttresses would yield a total of eighteen... and they do not even carry biblical names. From north to south they are known as Blinkwater Peak, Porcupine, Jubilee, Barrier, Valken, Kasteel, Poster, Woody, Spring, Slangolie, Corridor, Grootkop, Separation, Victoria, Grove, Llandudno Peak, Llandudno Corner and Hout Bay Corner.

Today's luxurious green roofed five-star Bay Hotel, on the left of the road, stands on the site of the original farmhouse.

The first private homes were built in 1828.

The journey continues...past the tantalising beach, restaurants and pavement cafés.

The road, hugging the Atlantic coast, rises slightly. The sea washes over massive flat rocks, the **'Groot Pannekoek'**, **'Klein Pannekoek'**, (Big and Small Pancake) and **'Geldkis'**. The 'Geldkis' ('Money Chest') brings to mind the ill-fated ship 'Huis te Crayestein' which foundered on this rock, carrying pay chests....all but three were recovered.

You are travelling along the drier, western side of Table Mountain where the average annual rainfall measures only about 700mm. The winter rains, and

Cape Town falls into the winter rainfall area, do not favour the Atlantic side.

About 1 km outside Camps Bay, marked by a bus-stop, steps lead off to the left, up the slope, to the **Bellsfontein Karamat**, the sacred tomb of **Nureelmobeen**. He was a Malay saint who, according to traditional belief, escaped from Robben Island and came to live and die there.

A mosque in the Bo-Kaap

THE FIRST MUSLIMS IN SOUTH AFRICA

The forebears of the large South African Muslim community reached the Cape's shores as political refugees, exiles or slaves from far flung places such as Java, Bali, India, China and Malaysia.

Towards the end of the 17th century an influential exile landed. He was Sheik Yussuf, brother of the King of Goa, Macassar. Born in 1626, he moved to Bantam on the island of Java to spread the Islamic faith. When the King of Goa abdicated in favour of his younger son, Sheik Yusuf, a deeply religious man, became embroiled in the political affairs as the king's son was totally in the power of the Dutch East India Company, the DEIC. Both the ageing king and the sheik feared for the independence of Bantam. Aided by the English, the old king made a vain bid to regain his throne. The failure led to England's withdrawal from the fight which the sheik alone simply could not win. He sought refuge in a remote village, accompanied by a few loyal followers. Fate dealt him a dismal blow when the Dutch captured his daughter; to safeguard her well-being, the sheik surrendered to the Dutch governor. Many years he languished in prison in Batavia, still loved and respected by the people of Bantam.

The Dutch feared an uprising to free the sheik and moved him first to Sri Lanka and then, in 1694 to the Cape. He landed on board the 'Voetboog' in Table Bay, accompanied by a few friends and his two wives. He was a man of

Lion's Head & Little Lion's Head

unusual gifts, talent, strength and piety. He died in 1699 and was buried at Faure, near Macassar Beach on the False Bay coast.

The route continues past the Court Classique de Oudekraal hotel. On weekends this coastal stretch which, from Oude Kraal to Llandudno has been declared a marine reserve, is a favourite spot for divers exploring the sea bed around the shipwrecked 'Antipolis'. In the 1970's she was being towed to the scrapyard in the East, when a fierce storm snapped the towing rope. The 'Antipolis' was washed ashore and left to disintegrate here. During low tide remains of the wreck are still visible.

The road (M6) sweeps steadily uphill. Below, **LLANDUDNO** with its sandy beach nestles at the foot of Little Lion's Head, about 440m high. Once you have crossed over the nek, the view changes dramatically. The **HOUT BAY** valley unfolds before you.

Over the centuries, Hout Bay, the 'Wooden Bay', once a thickly forested valley, lush with evergreen indigenous trees, fell victim to the axe and fires. But despite past and present day exploitation, the valley still exudes a rural character.

THE STRANDLOOPERS - PENINSULAR, KHOIKHOI AND AUTSHUMAO

Archeological finds confirm that the Hout Bay coast was already populated about 30 000 years ago, during the Later Stone Age. Delicately shaped ornaments of sea and ostrich egg shells have been found which may indicate that these people did not devote their entire life to the gathering of food. The sea provided for them: mussels, alikreukel, periwinkel and perlemoen made up their diet, as well as probably dune moles and tortoises. Stone implements were in use for crushing ochre to small crescents used in composite tools, as well as bone arrows and tortoise carapaces to fashion bowls.

The descendants of the Peninsular Khoikhoi became herders and were known as the Goringhaicona. One of their best known leaders at the time of first contact between them and the Europeans was Autshumao, also known as Harry.

In 1631, the English took Autshumao to Bantam in the East. Here he acquired a considerable knowledge of English and became the postal agent for the British. On his return, he lived several years on Robben Island. When the Dutch settled at the Cape, he acted as an agent between van Riebeeck's officials who were intent on stock bartering, and the Khoikhoi living further inland. These activities made him a wealthy stockowner. An expedition in 1655 to the outlying area of today's Malmesbury and Saldanha, revealed how other Khoikhoi were in fact prevented by Autshumao from dealing directly with the Dutch East India Company at the fort in Cape Town. All dealings had to go through him. Rival leaders finally succeeded in having him banished to Robben Island.

Soon after landing, rumours reached the ears of the early Dutch settlers that Portuguese had settled in this valley. Mindful of the threat such possibility posed to the young Dutch settlement, the Commander, Jan van Riebeeck, dispatched the sloop 'Verburgh' to investigate. No Portuguese were encountered, but instead, the crew made contact with Strandloopers, the Peninsular Khoikhoi.

The Hout Bay valley had been under cultivation for many hundreds of years. But only in 1681 were the first grants of land given to white settlers, a year after the government's proclamation that 'the free sawyers were forbidden to cut down any more yellow wood trees and that the forests at Hout Bay were to be reserved for the Company's use only'.

At that time the Peninsular Khoikhoi had moved further up the Disa river and the land that was first granted to Europeans became known as KRONENDAL.

On the downhill drive you pass the 'Suikerbossie' Restaurant, on the left, and enter the SOUTHERN PENINSULA. At the bottom of the road, the traffic lights offer an option:

OPTION 'A': To Mariners' Wharf and Harbour: *At the traffic lights continue straight, ignoring all turn-offs and junctions until the unmistakable Mariner's Wharf buildings near the beach are reached. Ample parking is available. An*

THE CAPE FUR SEAL

The Cape Fur Seal(Arctocephalus pusillus) belongs to the family Otariidae or 'eared' seals, which includes sea lions. They have small external ears, unlike the true seals Phocidae. The Cape Fur Seal is endemic to the south-western shore of southern Africa, distributed around 3000 km of coastline in 25 breeding and 9 non-breeding colonies. Nineteen breeding colonies are situated on small, rocky near-shore islands and six on the mainland. Almost 75% of all pups are born in the mainland colonies.

From the early 17th century, Dutch, French, British and American sealers began to hunt the seals, killing for skins, meat and oil. No exact records exist, but probably 23 island colonies became extinct as a result of this indiscriminate hunting. Today the seals are protected under the Seals and Seabirds Protection Act of 1973.

These intelligent, playful and inquisitive animals possess exceptional hearing under as well as above water. When diving, they close their nostrils and eyes which forces them regularly to the surface in order to breathe. Younger seals manage to stay under water up to 15 minutes, whereas their elders surface only every 30 minutes.

The average life expectancy is 20 years. The female matures faster than the male, bearing the first young at the age of four. The male reaches the reproductive age only between the ages of 8 and 12 years. In the mating season the male abstains from food and relies solely on fat reserves. End November, early December the female gives birth, usually to one pup. At six weeks, the pup makes its first tentative attempts to swim, but only at five or six months does it venture out alone. Lubberly on land, seals are skillful swimmers, reaching speeds of about 28 km/h. They feed mainly on fish and squid.

entrance fee is payable to enter the harbour. Here you can visit the very interesting **Sea Fisheries Museum,** do a little souvenir shopping or board a boat for one of the many trips offered to **Duiker Island.** The island is home to countless Cape Fur Seals.

At the end of the tour to the harbour, turn right again into Harbour Road and then turn right into Princess Road to reach the centre of the village.

OPTION B: via 'World of Birds Park':

Bear left at the traffic lights into Victoria Road (M6). Directions to the 'World of Birds' are given near the intersection with Valley Road.

After the visit to Africa's largest bird park of over 3000 birds, return to Victoria Road and turn left.

THE RED DISA – DISA UNIFLORA

The crimson red disa belongs to the orchid family. Growing from corms, the disa is a moisture loving flower usually found flowering on wet cliff faces or along streams. Today almost a rarity, it once carpeted Table Mountain. Although known as the 'Pride of Table Mountain', it is found all along the coastal belt of the southwestern Cape, through to the eastern Cape and in Natal. It grows 500 - 700 mm high and bears its hood shaped flowers at the top of a fairly long stem. It flowers from the end of December to about March. One of the earliest Cape botanists, Dr Rudolph Marloth, discovered that the red disa is pollinated by the 'Table Mountain Beauty' butterfly, the Meneris tulbaghia.

Shortly you cross over an insignificant looking white-washed low bridge spanning the Disa River. Mostly only a trickle of water finds its way to the sea, but heavy rains can render the Disa into a vengeful torrent, bringing devastation to the valley.

Continue until the T-junction with the Main Road, signposted 'Wynberg (M63)/Fish Hoek' (M6). Head for Fish Hoek!

Shortly, on the left, you'll have a peek of the graceful old **Kronendal Homestead** with its green shutters and thatched roof. For a fuller view of the building, stop and cross the road, being mindful of the traffic.

By 1681 a Willem Basson had settled in the valley, described by Jan van Riebeeck as *"having the finest forests in the world, containing timber as long, thick and straight as one could wish"*. His grant of land became known as 'Kronendal' ('Valley of the Crown'). After his death, the farm changed hands several times until it became the property, towards the end of the 18th century, first of the Bierman and then the van Helsdingen families. Under this new ownership, land and building were developed which attained gradually the appearance of a family farm. The building is believed to date back to 1800. All the timber utilised in the construction of the homestead was found by van Helsdingen among the drift wood on the beach.

Approaching the centre of the village, St. Andrew's Road turns off to the left, leading to the very interesting **Hout Bay Museum**. Continuing straight on, near the junction with Princess Road (if you took option A, you would join at this point) a colourful flea-and craft market draws the crowds over weekends.

The Main Road weaves through the village, past small boutiques and cafés, a modern shopping centre, past the tiny **Anglican Church of St. Peter's** on the left. It was built in 1895 by Walter Gurney. The first school in Hout Bay opened its doors on these premises.

Then, as you glimpse the beach again, the road curves and rises steadily. This is the start of the imposing **CHAPMAN'S PEAK DRIVE**, a project Construction of the remarkable pass, initiated by a former Administrator of the Cape, de Waal, began in 1915. Until then only an arduous and precipitous footpath linked Hout Bay to Noordhoek. The daunting task, even of surveying the route along sheer cliffs seemed impossible - but seven years later, the engineering feat was completed. This magnificent drive was opened by the Governor-General, Prince Arthur of Connaught in May 1922.

Look down onto the beach. You may spot a **'Leopard'** crouching on a rock, often mistaken for a mermaid. This engaging sculpture, created by the local artist Ivan Mitford-Barberton, was erected 1963 in memory of the leopards that once roamed the valley. The last one was spotted in 1936!
Not far from the statue, the ruins of an old jetty, a silent and weathered witness to the days of manganese mining can be detected.

MANGANESE MINING IN HOUT BAY

In 1880 a company was established to explore the manganese wealth in the Cape Town area. Ten years later mining started on the slopes of Constantiaberg. High above the sea, adits were driven into the hills. Six levels of open-face mining bear witness to the intense effort made to mine the narrow, manganese carrying vein. Some of the passages reached depths of over 60 metres. But the labour seemed somehow sabotaged by the means devised to transport the ore from the mountain slopes to the waiting ships below. The miners laid a 750 m long chute down the steep slope to the jetty far below and heaved the manganese into the chute. Rumours still circulate that mining ended abruptly when one day too much ore hurtled down the chute, crashing right through the waiting ship's bottom and sinking her. But divers have yet to come across a wreck! The truth is that the lack of sufficient reserves, the decreasing grade of ore and transportation problems probably forced the company to close its doors in 1911.

FROM HOUT BAY TO KOMMETJIE

Chapman's Peak Drive

Chapman's Peak Drive winds across the mountain face below **Constantiaberg** (937m) recognisable by the TV mast. On the far side of the bay, the colourful fishing and pleasure harbour nestles at the foot of the Sentinel and Karbonkelberg.

Shortly you reach the ruins of the **East Fort**, on the left.

As there is good parking, why not explore the ruins?

During the **First British Occupation** (1795 - 1802), the new authorities were keenly interested in Hout Bay. They considered the bay a good alternative anchorage point in bad weather conditions. But they feared above all that the vast bay, so distant from the Castle, could be a landing place for hostile forces. Anxious of such possibility, General Craig had a fortified blockhouse erected. It measured 8,5 metres in length and 6 metres in width. The three-storey building was equipped with magazines and water tanks. Below the fort stood a battery of five 18-pounders and five wooden huts for accommodation.

No hostile shot was ever fired from the fort, no invading force ever entered the bay. So, in 1827 the Cape government ordered the dismantling of the East

Fort. Some of the trunnions of the original cannon bear dates between 1756 and 1759 and on some the V.O.C. monogram can be seen. Others bear devices that suggest that they were French guns brought in by the French Pondicherry regiment, during the French garrison at the Cape from 1781 to 1784.

Chapman's Bay is one of the first English place names mentioned in South Africa. The 'English Pilot' states in 1703 that *'Chapman's Chance is a very good harbour, and lieth in the latitude of 34 degrees, 10 minutes lying within the southwest point, under a little hillock, close by the shore on the S.S.W. side, like a table, then named Hout Bay'.* Apparently an English ship, the 'Consent' was becalmed and the captain had sent one of his crew, John Chapman across to the mainland to find fresh water and safe shelter.

Noordhoek Peak (763m) and **Chapman's Peak** (582m) rise on the left. Across the bay the Sentinel stands guard. Chapman's Peak was the first mountain climbed by the then newly formed Mountain Club of South Africa in 1893. Across the bay, the **Sentinel** stands watch.

Numerous wonderful viewing and picnic sites invite you to pause and marvel. At the highest point of the pass a small footpath leads to the top of the hill, with sweeping views over Hout Bay, Chapman's Bay and Noordhoek Beach

The Sentinel guarding Hout Bay

Long Beach

across to Kommetjie. On the downhill stretch of Chapman's Peak Drive the scenery changes dramatically. The almost vertical, sheer cliffs of Chapman's Peak, seemingly close enough to touch, plunge into the sea, and the road cuts through sedimentary dark coloured layers of sandstone and the lighter, grey-coloured granite, exposed below the road.

Be ready with your camera! As the road winds downhill, the dazzling, seemingly endless stretch of white sands of Noordhoek beach will take your breath away. How inviting the sand, how awesome the rolling waves, how brilliant the turquoise blue water below. This is the widest beach in the Peninsula, and measures about 8 km in length, stretching across to Kommetjie. Known as **'Het Lange Strand'** ('Long Beach'), the beach is nonetheless dangerous for swimming because of strong backwash and currents. Not too dangerous though for surfers, given the right conditions, and definitely popular with riders and walkers.

Gazing across the beach, something square and dark in the sand, at the far end of the beach may catch your eye. These are the sad remains of the ship **'KAKAPO'**.

The 'Kakapo' ran aground in 1900, on May 26. Sailing on her maiden voyage from England to New Zealand, she had taken on coal Cape Town. During her onward journey, the Kakapo fell foul of a nor'westerly gale. There seems to have been no explanation as to why she drifted onto the sand at Noordhoek

Beach, the 'happening' being referred to as mysterious as the Captain refused to comment, other than saying that he had mistaken Danger Point for Cape Point, and thus made too early a turn.

Damage was not too great, yet salvage attempts to refloat her failed and the ship was finally left high and dry for wind, waves and weather to batter her. At the time, the 'Kakapo' turned into an instant and bountiful 'fish market' for the local children. Clasping their fishing lines, they sat patiently on the edge of the hold, waiting for the tide to fill it up. And with the outgoing tide many a fish got trapped and landed eventually on the supper table.

For quite a while, the 'Kakapo' remained reasonably intact, but time took its toll. She was gradually dismantled. Many parts were re-used, such as the iron staves with which a barrier between the sand dunes at Fish Hoek and the sea was built, to keep the Main Road clear of drift sand.

During World War I, much of the iron was removed for re-cycling into weaponry. Over the years, most of the exposed bodyworks rusted away, and today only a few weather worn ribs stick out of the sand. In the early 1960's she enjoyed one final moment of glory: the producer of the film **'Ryan's Daughter'** decided to shoot some parts of the film on Noordhoek Beach and dressed her up for the occasion. Her sides were touched up and a funnel of papermache added; she was made to look like a ship that had just gone aground, and so she was left until wind and weather took their toll once more.

The 'Kakapo' was not alone to succumb to the elements and, in this case perhaps to misjudgement. Chapman's Bay was the scene of many shipping disasters.

The journey continues.

The road (M6) unhurriedly descends into the wide **Noordhoek Valley** flanked to the north by the **Noordhoek** and **Kalk Bay Mountains**, and to the south by **Brakkloofrand** and **Elsies Peak**.

You pass the charming **'Noordhoek Farm Village'** where you can enjoy a break and browse in the delightful boutiques and craft shops. Then you reach the intersection with the M64, **Ou Kaapse Weg**. Turn right, drive past the outskirts of Sun Valley to the left, past the modern shopping complex until you reach the traffic lights. Here street vendors offer their goods. On a sunny weekend you can almost buy anything from a second-hand motor car to oranges, Windhoek salami, braai wood and coathangers.

Don't be confused by the many directional options: head right for **Kommetjie** *along the M65. For a moment the sea disappears from view as the road leads past the* **Masiphumelele** *township. This is a busy road with heavy pedestrian traffic. Take care.*

Shortly you reach **OCEAN VIEW**, established during the apartheid era for the coloured community.

The Ocean View site was part of the old Imhoff's Gift Farm, and expropriated for the construction of the township. The first residents who had been forcefully removed during the apartheid era from their homes in Simon's Town and elsewhere, were settled in Ocean View during the early 1960's. A bleak future awaited them as there were no schools, churches, shops, transport, sporting or entertainment facilities, scarcely any employment opportunities and the distance to and from the Fish Hoek railway station enormous.

For years, a group of women from Kommetjie and Simon's Town drove children to school or pensioners to Fish Hoek on pension day to collect their money from the Post Office, do a little shopping or take them to the hospital before Ocean View had its own clinic, shops, schools and post office.

Just outside Ocean View, ignore the signpost pointing to a left-turn off to **CAPE POINT**. *This route along Slangkop Road is marginally shorter but by-passes Kommetjie.*

On the way to Kommetjie, a chapel and cross dominate the hill on your left. To view the **Rubbi Chapel**, a famous landmark in Kommetjie, turn left into Rubbi Road.

THE RUBBI CHAPEL

Rubbi, of Italian origin and a Roman Catholic, was one of the earliest permanent residents of Kommetjie. He died in 1942. His widow wished to remember him in a befitting manner. She purchased four plots on the mountain slopes, on what is now Rubbi Road, and with great determination, set about planning the building of the Memorial Chapel and the adjoining tomb, also now known as the mausoleum. This, at a time, when the village of Kommetjie boasted only a sprinkling of houses and numbered very few Catholics. The then Roman Catholic Bishop of Cape Town, Bishop Henneman implored her to build a church in some other area that had a more desperate need of one, but to no avail. It had to be in Kommetjie!

Whilst her gardener planted and tended young olive trees on the surrounding plots, she left for Italy to buy the floor marble, the marble slabs, depicting the 12 stations of the cross, the painting for the ceiling and other equipment required, including the bells. By the time she returned, the building was virtually completed, spire and all. But then the troubles started.

Many of the marbles had been broken in transit. An expert was brought out from Italy who spent months repairing the damage.

During that time, a Kommetjie resident woke one morning to the loud ringing of bells. It seemed very close to her house. Rushing outside, huge scaffolding, like a jungle gym, constructed to the builder's specifications of the spire, stared at her, with bells merrily swinging to and fro.

On this wooden contraption the bells were being tested for the width of their swing. It turned out to be too wide for the completed tower which had to be demolished and rebuilt to meet the requirements of the bells.
The mausoleum was built of beautifully dressed local Table Mountain sandstone. In 1988 it had to make way for a second church, the chapel having been well outgrown by the present congregation.

In the early days of chapel worship, the congregation embraced Mrs Rubbi, her Italian house staff, the chauffeur, Sophia the housemaid and the Chef.

Once a month they arrived, having borrowed a priest to conduct a mass in the chapel. In time, however, an Order was founded to take over the responsibility for the Rubbi Chapel. These were the **Norbetines** who left the Belgian Congo when it gained its independence in 1961.

This led to the building of a small convent to accommodate Father Sweeds and his novitiates. Father Sweeds, a humble Christian and humanitarian was widely respected and loved by all people. His tireless efforts were also responsible for the building of a church and a Hall in near by Ocean View.

After this short detour, return to the Main Road which leads through the outskirts of **KOMMETJIE**, once a tranquil seaside village, today a lively, fast growing community. The earliest houses date back to around 1900.

Kommetjie means 'Little Bowl' because of the numerous natural inlets in the rocks, subsequently developed into a large tidal pool.

Until World War II, Kommetjie remained largely unknown and undeveloped. The absence of electricity until 1939, piped water until about 1953, lack of proper roads and facilities for sports and entertainment of any kind probably was probably the reason.

But through the war, Kommetjie moved into the spotlight.

Masses of troops passed through Cape Town. Refugees from the East, particularly Indonesia and Malaysia, poured into South Africa, hoping for a sea passage back home. For months on end they waited and accommodation was desperately short. Surveys of outlying suburbs and villages determined how many holiday homes, spare rooms and outhouses were available for temporary housing. Small hotels like the one at Kommetjie (now a rehabilitation centre) were eventually commandeered by the Army and the Navy. Thus many foreigners moved into Kommetjie, and they were visited by, and taken under the wing of Capetonians who now began to discover the village.

Kommetjie Lighthouse

Soon the road begins to climb, affording good views of the Atlantic, Soetwater Recreational grounds (Witsand) and the Slangkop Lighthouse.
The often dangerously high and rough seas along this stretch of coast have claimed many a victim. One of them, the **'CLAN MONROE'** ran aground in August 1905 and settled on a rocky shelf just below the Kommetjie Lighthouse. The other, the **UMHLALI** ran aground, also near the Lighthouse, in 1910.

SLANGKOP (KOMMETJIE) LIGHTHOUSE

The lighthouse on Slangkop Point was completed just before the war in 1914, but only commissioned in March 1919. The reason? Its light would have illuminated the neighbouring radio station, erected in 1910. The radio station with its three enormously high masts was the most important, if not the only means, of controlling shipping in the southern hemisphere during the First World War. It therefore needed protection and a military camp was established close by on the opposite side of the road. Three houses were built immediately below the Lighthouse for the staff and a terrace of three, slightly further away for the wireless operators. The Lighthouse has a range of 34 sea miles. It is 41 high metres and electricity was introduced in 1936 when also the intensity was increased to 16 000 000 CD, which in turn was reduced to 5 000 000 CD in 1974 when a 1,5 kW lamp was fitted. It is built of steel.

'CLAN MONROE'

The distress signals of the 'CLAN MONROE' were picked up, and a rig and breeches-buoy arrived from nearby Simon's Town. Sadly the ropes of the breeches buoy had not been tested before the first man climbed into the buoy - they broke as he was being winched through the breakers, and he drowned. The rest of the crew were all brought ashore safely.

Several of the stokers stood dumb as they waded ashore, their cheeks swollen. Was it their lack of English, or were they shocked into silence? Their rescuers soon found out: when they finally opened their mouths, they coughed out money, in hard coins,- the wages they had hoped to take home!

During the 1970's a lifeboat, operated by two men, used to take off and head out to sea towards the Lighthouse, and disappear around the corner - always on a calm, quiet day, and always at low tide. They were obviously not fishing, but diving down to the Clan Monroe to retrieve thick copper cables. Eventually they also collected a large, square copper boiler which they anchored in the bay for the night, intending to collect it the following day: but alas, when they returned, others had got there before them and carried their prize away.

'UMHLALI'

The 'UMHLALI' with her mixed cargo broke up and surrendered everything to the currents, much to the delight of the locals at the time. Kommetjie beach turned into a treasure trove. Of course, customs officials investigated but apparently were only interested in the whisky and brandy casks that littered the beach: they were claimed by the government. But everything else was free for all! Children and fishermen alike dug up items, collected and dragged boxes up the sandy beach. Cases of 'Lifeboy' soap, tinned pea soup and herring in tomato sauce. Candles washed up in the surf, as the containers were smashed on the rocks and the contents drifted out. What a spectacle to watch the breakers curl over with masses of candles, then dumping them on the shore. Then, as the waves receded, the local children made a dash for the candles and scurried back to safety before the next breaker rolled in. This way almost 1200 candles were stored in the loft of one of the homes, many of them short and fat at the bottom, to fit into the holders of pianos. All shapes and sizes were welcome, as Kommetjie knew no electricity at the time.

Other spoils gathered from among the rocks or the mountains of kelp on the beach were several balls of material; bathing costumes and frocks were made of these; a huge leaden cask, badly dented, containing rolls of hair-ribbon of all widths and colours, much to the disappointment of the boys who had worked hard to drag the cask up the dunes; there were hairbrushes, hand-sewn red leather cricket balls, golf balls, tennis racquets, and croquet mallets. There were fountain pens, toys - stiff toys, like cats and teddies, with ribbons round their necks and little bells hanging on them; drums, much battered and often difficult to remove from between the rocks, containing beautiful snowy lard; cases and cases of flat, green jewellery boxes, silk-lined; cases of white fancy collars and bows, the latter on small safety pins, such as elderly ladies pinned onto the front of their high-necked blouses. 'Jabots' they were called; lifebelts and driftwood, ships lanterns, buoys, hold covers... the lifebelts were made of white canvas, stitched into square sections and stuffed with flat bits of cork. They had shoulder straps, covered the chest and the back and tied up at the sides.

FROM KOMMETJIE TO CAPE POINT

The twisting, turning road traverses **Slangkop** (175m) and then descends to the coast again near **Witsand** (White Sands). Witsand, during the apartheid years reserved for the coloured community, has developed into a prime caravan and camping site.

Crayfish factory

The curious construction on **Witsand Island** is a crayfish processing factory for the export market.

Shortly the Slangkop Road coming from Ocean View, joins in on the left.

For a while the road hugs the coast; the hills, such as **Platkop** and **Vlooiberg**, reach average heights of 370 metres. Soon another village welcomes you: **SCARBOROUGH**. Situated at the mouth of the **Schusters River**, this sleepy village is a favourite with fishermen and comes to life in the summer holiday months. On the left you pass a couple of restaurants; one, the Camel Rock Restaurant takes its name from the peculiarly shaped sandstone rock, Scarborough's landmark, which can be seen diagonally across the road, on the right.

As you continue, look across towards the ocean for your first glimpse of the Cape Point Nature Reserve.

The road forks shortly: the **Red Hill Road** *(M 66), a scenic drive directly over the mountains to Simon's Town, branches off to the left. It ascends diagonally the slopes of the 330m high* **Langeberg***, then traverses the plateau, before descending in sharp bends into Simon's Town, there to join the coastal road (M4).*

At the fork, turn right, continuing on the M65. Don't break too hard when you see long-necked giraffe, massive hippos and elephant crafted from wood or stone confronting you: any last minute souvenir shopping can now be done here, or again near the gates of the Nature Reserve - but you may just need your own special cargo plane!

Along the way, past windswept eucalyptus trees, **ostriches** pace gracefully through the fields of the **Cape Point Ostrich Farm**, on the left. This exclusive breeding farm allows no riding or racing of the birds, but interesting tours are organised. Refreshments and light ostrich meat lunches are available, and again a little shopping in the farm's exquisite boutiques.

OSTRICHES (Struthio *camelus*). Throughout the ages, the ostrich has attracted man's interest.

In many parts of the world, paintings of ostriches have been discovered: on rocks in Fort Djanet in the Sahara; on eucalyptus trees in Australia, sketched by the aborigines; in cave shelters of the nomadic San of southern Africa; on the sarcophagus of pharaoes in ancient Egypt.

Roman and Greek helmets were resplendent with their feathers, whilst Assyrian kings were attended by their servants with ostrich feather wands.

Queen Nefertar ('The Charming Companion') sported brilliant headplumes, as did the royal soldiers of Pharaoes and the High priests.

The Phoenicians buried their dead with an ostrich egg on the knee, and eggs adorned the coptic church spires in Egypt. The San used the egg for water storage in the desert sands, or crafted dainty ornaments from the egg's hard shell.

Beloved by some, derided and even feared by others: some Arabian tribes believed the bird to be a re-incarnation of evil; in 300 BC the tyrant Firmius harnessed them to chariots and Emperor Gordian III had some painted red for amusement.

The South African ostrich, the biggest flightless bird, is related to the emu and kiwi, the South American rhea and the cassowary. Ostrich farming had been practised in northern Africa for a long time, but it was generally believed that the bird would not mate in captivity. This false belief was proved wrong by South African farmers in the middle of the 19th century.

The cock, easily recognized by his comely black and white feathers, grows to about 2 m high. The hen appears a little more scruffy in her brownish feathers. Yet, as both sit on the egg for breeding, their feathery attire is the perfect camouflage, as the male guards the eggs at night until the clutch is complete, and the female during the day. For a nest, the male bird scrapes a hollow of about 1,5m in diameter in sandy soil. Breeding, depending on rainfall, occurs all months.

Though perhaps less attractive, the female is earnestly courted by the male. Spreading his wings and gracefully dancing before her, he seeks her acceptance which she shows by kneeling before him.

The hen lays the first egg, which is much smaller than the later eggs, about 14 days after mating. She crushes this always infertile egg and swallows the shell for a natural supply of calcium. Thereafter she lays an egg, a deep creamy yellow, about every second day, until a clutch of 12 to 15 eggs has been laid. On breeding farms this number is drastically increased to about 35 eggs as eggs are continually removed from the nest. An ostrich egg weighs about 1kg and is the equivalent of 24 chicken eggs. After an incubation of 42 days, the chicks hatch. Until the age of 14 months, male and female are indistinguishable from each other with their scrawny feathers. They reach maturity from the age of about $2^{1}/_{2}$ to 3 years.

Under natural conditions, an ostrich's life span is up to 40 years, but can grow older on breeding farms.

Though normally docile, the bird can be aggressive during the mating season when the skin on the two-toed feet and the beak of the male turns reddish pink. It is incidentally, the only two-towed bird in the world.

The ostrich does not kick backwards. It lifts the foot and with a downward kick tears the victim with its frightful toenails. As it reaches speeds of up to 75 km/h, often running with its wings spread wide for balance, one would be ill advised to run away from an attacking bird. It is best to lie flat on the ground in the hope that the ostrich would either run over you, or at worst, just sit on you..bearing in mind that a male bird can weigh well over 120kg!

Its appetite is healthy, devouring anything from lucerne, maize, berries, seeds, succulent plants, small insects to cooldrink tins, bangles and necklaces. Bright shiny jewellery is highly prized by the bird.

Though unable to fly, the ostrich can swim and go for long periods without water.

Let's shift attention away from the ostriches, to the **eucalyptus trees**, also known as blue gums, lining the route.

These trees were imported from Australia during the 19th century, at a time when the indigenous forests had succumbed to unscrupulous felling or fire. The rapidly developing country needed wood for mining shafts, railway sleepers, fencing poles and, later telephone and electricity poles. The import of fast growing, hardwood aliens was, at the time an obvious solution. As the blue gums are also fire resistant, their appeal was unlimited. Sadly, little was known about their destructive forces: a fully grown tree drains up to 250 litres of water per day from the soil. In an arid country like South Africa this tree along with many other invader plants turns into a rapacious destroyer of the indigenous flora.

Slow down as you pass the colourful souvenir stalls, just before a sharp turn to the right for the **CAPE OF GOOD HOPE NATURE RESERVE.** After you have paid the entrance fee, the first grand view of **FALSE BAY** welcomes you to the park. The distance from the gate to Cape Point is 13 km.

The road swings around **Rooihoogte** (300m) on the right, and gradually descends onto the vast plateau sloping from east to west towards the Atlantic coast. To the east, the backs of **Judas Peak** (331m), **Die Boer**(325m), **Paulsberg** (370m), drop abruptly into the sea. Thickly growing shrubs, particularly leucodendrum, leucospermum, restios and everlastings are woven into a seemingly endless flowery carpet.

Paulsberg, Die Boer, Judas Peak seen from the south

FYNBOS

*The Afrikaans word fynbos means 'fine bush'. It fittingly describes the fine-leaved heathland vegetation which grows on the infertile soils of the Cape mountains and near the coast. It is the most extensive and species-rich vegetation in the **Cape Floristic Kingdom**. The most distinct members of fynbos are the **ericas** or heath, the many reeds of the **restio** family and the **proteas**. Fynbos has adapted to the Cape's wet winters and the intense, desiccating summer winds. Joining the protea, erica and restio families, are orchids, gladioli; irises and many others.*

The Cape of Good Hope Nature Reserve, established in 1938 at Africa's most south-westerly tip, covers nearly 7750 hectares. The wind-swept plains, sandy shores and rocky outcrops shelter over 1800 species of plants, many of them endemic, more than 50 species of mammals, over 40 species of reptiles and amphibians as well as about 250 species of birds.

Why is the Cape blessed with such a wealth and variety of flowers?

In part it may be explained by the fact that, although the Cape suffered under deep layers of ice about 110 million years ago, it was never again glaciated after flowering plants began to evolve. Consequently plant communities developed and matured in this region, whilst vast areas of the northern hemisphere still lay under deep ice-sheets. Naturally, over the ages some plants vanished because of further climatic changes, but others adapted and survived.

Additional factors may be the varying geological ages of plant habitats and the climate. Geologically speaking, the Cape is blessed with young coastal plains as well as ancient peaks. The sea levels too fluctuated in the past, thus isolating the Cape Peninsula sporadically, which may explain the abundance of endemic plants.

King Protea, South Africa's national flower

The Cape delights in a Mediterranean climate in the west, with winter rainfall changing to all year rainfall going eastwards, and finally becoming a summer rainfall region near Port Elizabeth.

Lastly, the soil also adds to the profusion of flowers.

Restio

Erica

The infertile sandstone soils of the mountains support true **'fynbos'**, a heathland vegetation type, whereas two non-heathland shrublands, known as 'renosterveld' and 'strandveld' flourish on the richer soils of the lowland areas, where grasses and bulbuous plants are more common.

The wealth of flowers qualifies part of the Cape as one of the floristic kingdoms of the world, albeit the smallest in area.

The main road to the Point passes numerous turn-offs.

The first leads off to the right, to **'Olifantsbos'** (Elephants' Bush), at the foot of Rooihoogte. At Olifantsbos you find a lovely beach and, if time allows, you could embark on a **shipwreck walk**, leading to the **'Thomas T. Tucker'** wreck. The ship foundered in 1942. Or you walk the circular route to **Sirkels Vlei** where you may spot game.

Thomas T. Tucker

44

About 4 km from the entrance gates, the Circular drive starts, branching off to the west towards the Atlantic Ocean.

Though the **Circular Drive** brings you back to the main road of the reserve, it allows for a short detour to **'Gifkommetjie'**. Here you can enjoy brilliant views of rolling waves, sandy beaches from a view-platform. An easy, but steep path descends to the beach.
Back on the main road, about 2km further on, a gravel road to the left heads for **'Bordjiesdrif'**, meaning 'Little Plate Reef' on the False Bay coast. Just before reaching the parking area and tidal pool at Bordjiesdrif, another gravel road to the left is marked **'Black Rocks'**. It takes you to an old lime kiln that was used to make lime for mortar in the days when buildings were still put up here. Further on, the road passes close to Paulsberg and ends finally in a small car park. From here a fairly long walk takes you to **Venus Pool**, a series of large crystal clear rock pools.

You will also drive past the **Vasco da Gama** beacon surveying False Bay, a large white cross. It serves both as a memorial to the Portuguese seafarer and as a navigational beacon.

This stretch of coast is wild and rocky with deep water inshore, ideal for fishing.

Back along the main road, the old buildings of the former Smith Farm, the last owner of the farm before it became a Nature Reserve, to the left, are passed and the small **Information Office** to the right. Next to it stands a

Vasco da Gama Beacon

monument to **Sidney Harold Skaife**, a leading force behind the creation of the Cape of Good Hope Nature Reserve.

A little further on, again to the left, a turn-off leads to **Buffel's Bay**, the largest picnic and braai area in the park, with magnificent views across the Bay, the mountains and towards Cape Point. You probably will not be able to resist a short stroll on the magnificent beach. Swimming is dangerous, but a tidal pool will cool you down.

Dias Beacon

In the parking area you may notice a smaller *padrao*, stone cross, erected in 1988 by the Portuguese community commemorating Bartholomeus Dias.

There are launching facilities for fishermen.

Driving on, to the right the signpost **'Platboom'** steers you to another cross, the **Dias Cross**, erected in the mid 1960s in honour of Bartholomeus Dias.

DIAS AND DA GAMA BEACONS

The beacons were designed by Sydney Hunter and unveiled in 1965. They serve as a memorial and as navigational beacons; a ship in False Bay, once aligned with these beacons and in conjunction with the beacon above the Simon's Town Golf Course, is warned of the submerged Whittle Rock, a hazard to shipping. The beacons resemble a padrao, a monument erected by the Portuguese sailors in newly discovered land. The padrao showed the cross of Christ, the royal Portuguese Coat of Arms and an inscription stating when and by whom it was raised. King John II, nephew of King Henry the Navigator was the first to order their erection. They testified to Portuguese sovereignty and Christianity. To off-set the whit.e beacon against the horizon, Dias Beacon is painted black on the eastern side.

If you continue to Platboom, you will discover a magnificent beach and almost all year round, rich birdlife.

Cormorants, Egyptian geese, herons, egrets, Sacred ibises and African Black Oystercatchers roost peacefully on the rocks, side by side, until the shrill cry from the Blacksmith Plover alerts them of approaching danger.

Oystercatchers

The African Black Oystercatcher's survival is threatened. The bird is recorded on the red data list. They breed in summer, laying their eggs between December and February, and chicks appearing from January to about May. Both parents take care of the 32 day incubation and a normal clutch numbers one to two, rarely three eggs. Though skillful in prising open shells, their favourite food, and indefatigable workers to lever limpets from the rocks, the oystercatchers are very sluggish as nest builders. The nest is a mere, shallow depression in the sand, close to some dried seaweed or flotsam and jetsam from the sea, and often below the spring high-tide mark. No care is taken to conceal the nest or the clutch, vulnerable to predators, human feet and unfortunately elsewhere along our shores to motor cars.

The journey continues. The next turn-off to the left, indicates **'Rooikrans'**, a superb line fishing spot.

Although more than thirty species are known at the Reserve's coast, the most common species are Hottentot, Galjoen and Yellowtail.

To line fishermen, the **Rooikrans Ledges** are unsurpassed as deep water is accessible from only very few spots along the shore.

The fishermen wind their way downhill along a rough, hazardous track at the foot of **Vasco da Gama Peak**, along the cliff edge to the ledges, a mere couple of metres above the sea.

YELLOWTAIL

Yellowtail are found in temperate southern oceans. In South African waters they migrate up to 50 km per day in enormous shoals along the south and east coasts. Spawning occurs off the coast of Natal in the summer and autumn until April or May. It is a fast growing fish, reaching 40 cm in the first year. A fully grown yellowfish can weigh up to 10 kg. The biggest caught tipped the scales at 60 kg.

We leave the fishing for a while and continue along the main road until the turn-off to the right is reached, directing you to the **CAPE OF GOOD HOPE**.

Gently descending towards the Atlantic coast whilst waves break over the rocks and roll on to the sand, you pass **Neptune's Dairy**, popular with skin divers in search of crayfish and perlemoen.

PERLEMOEN

It is a member of the widely distributed abalone family. Its large, flat shell is characterised by a row of holes along its left side. Through these holes, water products and deoxygenated water are expelled. It is slow growing: in the cold waters off the coast at the Cape of Good Hope it can take a dozen years or more to grow to 12 cm in size. Spawning occurs in spring and summer; an incredible 15 million eggs may be produced at one time by the bigger individuals.
The name perlemoen stems from the Dutch paarlemoer, meaning mother-of-pearl. It has formed part of the diet of the indigenous people for thousands of years.
Over exploitation has led to the introduction of a rigorous quota system for commercial and recreational fishermen. Licences are required.

A few hundred metres further on you reach, literally, the end of the road: the **CAPE OF GOOD HOPE**, the continent's **most south'westerly point**, situated at **34° 21'25"South**.

View across to Cape Point

Now its time for a momentous photograph! You have finally reached the Cape with all its magic. To capture it all, follow an easy board-walk (15 to 20 minutes) uphill to a breathtaking view-site. En route a sign-post directs you to this site. By all means also explore the track off to the left, but do not persist to the end of this spectacular path, as it winds it way across towards **CAPE POINT** - unless you have another car to meet you there! (this walk would take about 40 minutes).

As you scramble up and down, you will probably make the acquaintance of a curious little animal, basking lazily in the sunshine on the rocks, or scrambling away into narrow crevices. Frequently mistaken for rock rabbits, they are in fact rock hyraxes, or **'dassies'**.

DASSIES- ROCK HYRAX

Procavia capensis. This small, social and diurnal mammal adores scampering about on rocky outcrops, soaking up the sunshine, but is also known to live in antbears' caves. Generally, the surprisingly agile 'dassie', is a shy vegetarian. A glandular secretion keeps the sole of their thickly padded feet sticky, which helps to give them a foothold on steep, smooth rock surfaces. Their unique flexible ribs allow them to almost completely flatten their bodies. They are distant relatives of the elephant. The 'dassie' has a life expectancy of about 12 years. Usually, one to six young are born after an incubation of nearly 230 days. An adult weighs close to 4kg and measures 55 cm in length.
Dassies have many natural enemies, including jackals and eagles.
Each group urinates only in one place and after generations a dark brown crystalline substance forms. This was used by the Khoi and the early European settlers to make cough mixtures.

KELP OR SEAWEED

is prolific along the West Coast. Kelp absorbs the necessary nutrients from the surrounding water and therefore needs no roots. Its hollow stem is anchored to the rocky seabed. Long-armed 'leaves' extend from the top of these stems and float on the surface. Seaweed grows rapidly, up to 13mm per day in summer, and can reach 12 metres in length. Wherever it finds a suitable basis to which it can attach itself, the weed will grow. When fertile, each square centimetre of its blades can produce up to 10 000 spores per hour, the alga's reproductive units.
The depth to which kelp probes depends on the penetration of sunlight needed for photosynthesis. In clear water it can flourish up to 30 metres.
Seaweeds together with the phytoplankton, form the basis of the ocean's food chain. They are also important as a habitat for many other marine organisms.

THE ROCK LOBSTER

The Cape Rock Lobster - Jasus lalandii is plentiful along the west coast. Known as 'kreef' in Afrikaans, it is a very different crustacean from the crayfish caught in the northern hemisphere.
The season for catching opens mid-November and closes towards end of April, early May.

The eggs hatch towards October, when millions of tiny larvae float with the currents for about nine months. They molt and grow, and then, as transparent miniature lobsters, make their way inshore and find homes amongst the rocks and kelp, growing steadily and moulting their shells every year to accommodate their growing body in a larger covering.

Gazing across the turbulent sea in a south'westerly direction, you will notice white foam spraying over a submerged reef, known as the **Bellows**. Here the **'Lusitania'** came to grief.

The coastline near the Cape of Good Hope has claimed at least 24 ships; the remains of five of these are still visible along the beaches, the others have vanished beneath the ocean. It is the combination of currents and winds, together with large reefs and submerged rocks that led so many ships to their doom in the treacherous waters around the Cape of Good Hope Nature Reserve.

The Lusitania, a name-sake of the Cunard Liner torpedoed by a German U-boat off the southwest coast of Ireland in 1915, was a 5557 ton Portuguese steamer, launched in 1906. She was en route from Maputo (Moçambique).

Disaster struck for her 678 passengers and 122 crew on 18 April 1911. The captain had charted a course to give Cape Point a deliberate wide berth. Conditions were calm, though thick mist and low cloud hung over Cape Point. Then the mist lifted, and to his horror the ship's master realised that the Lusitania was heading for the lighthouse. Turning her to port he steered her out to sea and struck the 'Bellows'.

Distress rockets were fired, lifeboats lowered but no panic broke out aboard. The lighthouse keeper rushed down to the shore, waving a lamp, desperately seeking to stop people from rowing through the dangerous surf. But ignoring the warning, the boats steered towards the shore.. one capsized, drowning all aboard - but another 37 passengers were saved. Those that had heeded the lighthouse keeper's warning and remained off beyond the breakers were eventually all picked up by rescue vessels from Simon's Town.

Closer to the shore, brown kelp floating in the surf and winding itself around the rocks, attracts attention.

Competing with attention are the large sea-birds, huddled on the rocks, wings spread out: the **cormorants**.

Four of the thirty species known world-wide, have made the reserve their home. The Whitebreasted and Cape Cormorant even breed here.

The **Cape Cormorant** is endemic to the southern African coast. Thousands frequently come ashore on Dias Beach, that lovely sandy beach between the Cape of Good Hope and Cape Point. Or they sit on the rocks. The reserve counts about 2300 pairs. It builds an untidy but sturdy nest from sticks, lining it with fresh plant material, such as the grey, slightly aromatic stems of the creeping Heliochrysum.

Naturally you would like to linger at the Cape of Good Hope, but your journey must still take you to Cape Point. Retrace your route therefore up to the main road. Once at the T-junction, turn right.

Ignore the turn-off to Rooikrans, but take heed of the signs asking NOT TO FEED THE BABOONS.

Feeding the baboon, -*Papio ursinus* - means handing down the death sentence as they loose the ability to feed themselves.

For many, seeing the **Chacma baboons** foraging or at play is one of the highlights of a visit to the reserve.

The indigenous people called this extremely gregarious animal **'choachamma'** or **'choa kamma'**. The French zoologist, Baron Cuvier, adopted this name which became generally accepted as from 1819. The Chacma Baboon occurs as far north as Angola. The male attains an average height of 1,5m including the tail, and the female of 1,2m. The male weighs in at about 40 kg whilst the female tops the scales at only 20 kg. Adult males sport a tinge of yellow, mostly on the forehead. Females may be distinguished from other similar sized younger males by their brightly coloured ischial callosities on the rump, when in season. Males reach maturity at 8 years, and females at about 3 to 4 years.

In the Cape Point Nature Reserve most baboons are born between July and November, after a six month gestation. The baby is weaned after six to eight months. Mischievous and playful, the adults have their hands full with these juveniles....

Mid-morning and afternoon is taken up with feeding activities. Their diet is almost exclusively plant material: at the reserve over 100 different species are relished by them. But they are known to spice up their diet with delectable shellfish and other sea-life!

The tarred road climbs gently, (the few green-roofed houses on the slopes to the left were the former radar station). Finally you reach the large carpark at **CAPE POINT**.

To the right of the car park, one finds the toilet facilities, to the left a curio shop, restaurant, take-away, information centre, and the ticket office for the funicular railway. It is possible to buy a one way ticket. The funicular ride ends just below the old lighthouse. From here numerous stepped paths lead to the lighthouse and various view points. At the upper station another curio shop tempts the visitor.

Straight ahead and running parallel with the funicular, starts the well maintained and gently climbing footpath to Cape Point. On either side of the public facilities, signposts indicate the footpath leading across to the Cape of Good Hope. The same word of caution applies: a second vehicle is required at the other end, unless one returns the same way! Should you choose to walk along this path for a while (to escape the crowds!), a fork is reached after about 250 metres leading to a grand view of Cape Point. Return the same way.

Walking up to **Cape Point Peak** is enjoyable and invigorating. Allow close to 20 minutes, excluding the occasional pause for a photograph or catching your breath. To the west, Maclear buttress and Cape of Good Hope are visible; (Sir Thomas Maclear was a British astronomer who made scientific observations at the Cape in the 19th century). White sands on a pristine little beach where perhaps hundreds of cormorants are drying their wings separates Maclear buttress from Cape Point buttress - was it here that Dias's caravelle came ashore?

From the upper funicular station paths lead off to the restored old lighthouse and many other dazzling viewpoints. The new lighthouse can be spotted from a number of these viewpoints, but not from the old lighthouse.

THE LIGHTHOUSES

The first lighthouse at Cape Point was commissioned on 1 May 1860. It was constructed at a height of 249m above high water and used reflectors with a light of 1200 CD. In bad weather when visibility deteriorated, the old lighthouse disappeared into low cloud and mist. After the Lusitania had foundered on the rocks, a new lighthouse was constructed at a much lower level, 87m above the high water mark. The foundation stone was laid in 1914 and it was inaugurated on 25 April 1919. The original lamp was a paraffin vapour mantle. It was electrified in 1936. The light has an intensity of 10 million CD (candelas), making it the most powerful light on the South African coast. It gives three flashes at 3 second intervals from a revolving electric light visible 63 km out to sea. A fixed red subsidiary light points to Bellows and Anvil rocks. Since its installation, only two ships have come to grief in the vicinity.

Below, to the east (left) broods the vast expanse of **FALSE BAY**. Mariners of old frequently mistook **Hangklip** (453m), (The Hanging Cliff) on the tip of the eastern shores for the Cape of Good Hope and the bay became known as Cabo Falco, 'FALSE BAY'. Joining Cape Hangklip, which plunges steeply into the ocean are the **Buffelsberg** (843m), **Koelberg** (1013m) and the **Hottentots Holland Mountains** where the highest peak reaches 1337 metres.

Though not detectable, a lighthouse marks the entry into FALSE BAY at Cape Hangklip. It is unmanned and remote controlled from the Cape Point Lighthouse.

Now where do the oceans meet? Did you see that magical line separating the **Indian** from the **Atlantic Ocean**?

Cape Point

Of course you were deceived, but not intentionally, by the French naturalist, François Le Vaillant, and countless others after him. Le Vaillant noted in the late 18th century whilst in the Cape that *"Placed on the spot of the globe the most favourable perhaps for the grand spectacles, I had on my right the Atlantic and on my left the Indian, and before me the Southern Ocean which breaking with fury at my feet seemed as if desirous of attacking the whole chain of mountains and swallowing up my feet"...*

Capetonians appear somewhat reluctant to admit that **Africa's most southerly tip is Cape Agulhas**, situated about 120 km away along the east coast and stretching yet another 50 km further south into the ocean. It is there that the Indian and Atlantic Oceans encounter each other. But at least local pride is redeemed by the fact that two currents rendez-vous at Cape Point: the **AGULHAS** and **BENGUELA**.

The **Agulhas current** originates in the warm waters of the South Equatorial Current of the Indian Ocean. Meandering down the east coast of South Africa, it flows closely inshore before being deflected by the Agulhas Bank, a shallow submarine shelf stretching about 200 kilometres offshore slightly east of Cape Agulhas. Here, a whirlpool effect is created by the combined forces of wind and sea-bed topography, which forces the current back on itself. Some remnants of this warm Agulhas current, however, manage to push their way south, towards Cape Point, and there, drifting westward, they clash with the Benguela current. The Agulhas travels between 90 and 230 km per day. It evaporates comparatively easily, generates rains and is responsible for the lush green and fertile conditions of the east coast.

The **Benguela current**, born in the icy Antarctic, determines marine life and water temperatures at the west coast. Some 60 million years ago, from the regions of the ice in the Antarctic a cold current was spun off and flowed northwards towards the southern tip of Africa. The current brought with it natural riches of chemicals and minerals. Flowing northwards, it collided broadside with the warm Agulhas Current sweeping down the east coast of Africa.

The warm current, though weakening near Cape Point, remained strong enough to deflect the cold current westwards. The cold current hugged the west coast, killing off the original marine life. It was only 150 km in width, but this was sufficient to isolate the south-west coast from the far warmer Indian Ocean. Rainfall along the coast dwindled because cold water does not evaporate, and a transitionary desert developed in the south, with a full desert in the north (Namib).

The original marine forms either died from cold or fled the area for warmer waters. In their place, however, came cold water species, fewer varieties but vast quantities of pelagic fish (deep-water fish) like anchovies and pilchards. These little fish flourished on the rich stores of food in the cold current. The Benguela Current, moving at a speed of about 16 to 40km a day, carries with it 20 times the amount of nitrogen found in the Agulhas current. On this nitrogen feeds an immense population of plankton drifting with the current.

The plankton in their turn support vast shoals of pelagic fish, as well as crustaceans and shellfish known as filter feeders because they exist by sucking in plankton-rich water, feeding on the plankton and then expelling clean water.

Now that a long held belief has been shattered and you now know that the two oceans do not meet at Cape Point, perhaps you should check out other names, such as Cape of Good Hope?

CABO DE BOA ESPERANCA
CAPE OF GOOD HOPE

Dias, the famed Portuguese seafarer set sail in August 1487, ordered by King John II to establish a maritime route to the riches of the east. Accompanied by two other ships, one commanded by his brother, Dias's caravelle, the **'Sao Cristovao'**, reached Walvis Bay on the Namibian coast on 8 December. From here they pressed on in a southerly direction, but were delayed by fierce gales in a bay south of the Orange River.

Cape Point, False Bay, Buffels Bay

For thirteen days the winds raged, forcing them to keep their sails at half mast and blowing the small fleet far out to see, out of sight of land. When at last the wind calmed, the caravelles headed east, hoping to sight the west coast once more. Yet, having unwittingly rounded the Cape of Good Hope, they sailed east for a number of days before setting course for the north. And indeed, they sighted land, but on the east coast of Africa...Dias, now aware that he had successfully rounded the Cape, was keen to sail on. But his mariners revolted near today's Port Elizabeth and the fleet set sail for the homeward-bound journey. Some historians believe that Dias named the Cape the **CABO TORMENTOSO**, the Cape of Storms, but that King John re-named it 'Cape of Good Hope' because it gave the promise to the unlocking of the riches of the east.

THE CARAVELLE

The caravelle originates in the Mediterranean where, as from the 15th century, it was used by the Portuguese and Spaniards for their voyages of exploration and commerce along the African coast. Despite the lack of technical information on caravelles, intense research led to the construction of a replica, the 'Bartolomeu Dias' in the shipyards of Samuel & Silhos, at Vila do Condo, near Oporto. It can be seen in the Maritime Museum in Mossel Bay.

The hull of pine and oak, is 23,5m long and 6,62m wide at its broadest point. It has a displacement of about 130 tons, with about 37 tons of ballast, consisting of cement, granite and lead. The two-masted vessel carries two lateen sails. The grandsail measures 147m² and weighs 1,5 tons. The much smaller mizzen sail measures 73m².

During the quincentenary celebrations, the replica sailed from Portugal to the Cape, commemorating Dias's achievement.

But now it is time that you meet one of the giants of antiquity who is responsible for the raging storms at the Cape, described by Captain James Cook in the 1770's as 'the Cape is scarce ever free from storms a week together. The winds blow hard and on every side from the vast Southern Ocean, the waves of the sea rise to a height never seen or experienced in any part of Europe. The Bay of Biscay, turbulent as it is, has no billows that mount like those in this extensive ocean, the stoutest vessels are tossed and almost lifted to the skies'..

You have entered the realm of **ADAMASTOR**.

Adamastor, a semi-god was one of the Titans - the twelve children of Uranus and Gaea who personified heaven and earth respectively. Impatient with their submissive rôles, the Titans resolved to wrest power from the mighty gods and take control of heaven themselves. Their determination was no match, however, against the awesome power of Hephaestus and Heracles. The Titans were utterly crushed. Punishment befitting their treacherous deed awaited them: the all-powerful Zeus condemned the twelve brothers to be transformed into stone at the extreme limits of the earth. Atlas, one of the older was banished to the northern shores of Africa to carry the world on his shoulders, and his younger brother Adamastor banished to, and petrified, the farthest southern corner of Africa where now, deep inside Table Mountain, he whips up storms in his anger, looking for revenge.

This legend is told by the Portuguese poet **Luis Vaz de Camões** in his 1102 stanza-long poem **'Os Lusiads'** which praises the exploits of the Portuguese explorers in the East. The poet himself had travelled over a period of 17 years to and from from Portugal and India.

DIAS SHIPWRECK

Twelve years after his first rounding of the Cape, Dias sailed in the fleet commanded by Pedro Alvares Cabral. The fleet was heading far west and the coast of Brazil was sighted before it reset course back to the Cape. Weeks later, a terrifying storm lashed the fleet, shredding the full sails of nine of the vessels. Limping on, they at least remained upright, but Dias's vessel was not so fortuitous: she sank just off the Cape, taking him with her to a watery grave. The Cape he had claimed at last claimed him. Or was it Adamastor's revenge?

Who knows, perhaps there is a little truth in the story, as Dias, in his second attempt to round the Cape, twelve years later, suffered shipwreck in Table Bay.

Before leaving Cape Point, one more story must be told, the story of the **FLYING DUTCHMAN**, as it is so closely linked to Adamastor.

An elusive ghost ship haunts the restless waters off the Cape of Good Hope: The Flying Dutchman.

Could this be Dias's vessel, with its shredded sails and broken masts? Or is it Captain van der Decken's ship, the Dutchman who ran into a raging storm on his homeward bound journey in 1641? Desperate to reach home, he swore as his ship was sinking that he would round the Cape even if it meant sailing until Doomsday. Van der Decken perished, and his ship is seen struggling, fighting the waves..years later immortalised in Richard Wagner's opera of the 'Flying Dutchman'.

Sailors eagerly spin a yarn, and so it is told that whoever sighted this ship would perish, like Captain van der Decken. Superstition it might be, but then even the lighthouse keepers at Cape Point reported frequent sightings of the haunted ship; during World War II, German U-boat crews logged inexplicable sightings of sailing ships. But probably the most famous

VASCO DA GAMA

Da Gama set sail in 1497 with a fleet of four vessels including a supply ship, and rounded the Cape in November of the same year. Da Gama continued eastward, sailing up the east coast of Africa until he found an Arab pilot who guided him the 3000 kilometres across the ocean to India, arriving there in 1498.

recording of the ghost ship occurred in 1881. A young midshipman in the British Royal Navy, later to become King George V, noted in his diary that *'at 4 a.m the 'Flying Dutchman' crossed our bows. The lookout-man on the forecastle reported her as close to the port bow, where also the officer of the watch clearly saw her... a strange red light as of a phantom ship all aglow, in the midst of which light the mast, spars and sails of a brig 200 yards distant stood out in strong relief'.*

The journey continues, driving back to the entrance gates of the Reserve.

You may not sight the ghost ship but perhaps you will be rewarded with spotting some of the Reserve's animals. Look out for the **Bontebok, Cape Mountain Zebra, Eland, Red Haartebeest, Cape Grysbok, Mangoose** and the **Cape Angulated tortoise**.

An encounter with the **Bontebok** *'Damaliscus dorcas dorcas'* is fairly likely, but don't be disappointed if you fail to spot other larger mammals. Why is that?

Bontebok

Right from the start, battle lines were drawn. It was probably inevitable that botanists, ornithologists, ecologists and wildlife experts would clash over the development of the park.

Initially the dream of wild animals roaming free, prevailed. Black and Blue Wildebeest, Burchell's and Hartman's Zebra, Eland, Bontebok, Springbok, Red Hartebeest and others were introduced. To reach a compromise with the botanists who visualised a wildflower paradise, a fence, now removed, was erected which restricted the animals to the southern section of the park. Initially the antelopes appeared to thrive, but then began to display signs of ill health. The reserve turned out to be a short-lived haven for them. The reason? Apart from the Eland, all the other introduced animals were grazers, feeding almost exclusively on grass - something rare in fynbos vegetation.

Besides, many of the plants flourishing the reserve, lack essential nutrients. The survival of the introduced species could not be guaranteed. Years passed before these facts were recognised and accepted. In the end common sense finally won the day and the reserve developed essentially as a wilderness area. Thus the dream of an African wildlife park ended - the remaining animal populations are closely monitored today. If it is established that overgrazing takes place, for example, surplus animals are translocated to other reserves.

FROM CAPE POINT TO SIMON'S TOWN

After exiting the reserve, turn right at the T-Junction(M4) towards Simon's Town.

Smitswinkel Bay

The road serpentines downhill with dazzling views across False Bay. Within a short distance after leaving the reserve, you look down on **SMITSWINKEL BAY** ('Blacksmith Bay'), probably named after two oddly shaped rocks, the 'Anvil' and 'Bellow', a smithy's tools. A few houses, mostly holiday homes, dot the beach.

Whale spotting along the False Bay coastline is particularly rewarding. From about July to end of October the Southern Right Whales breach, lobtail, spyhop or simply 'sail' through the waters - an awesome sight.

THE SOUTHERN RIGHT WHALE
EUBALAENA AUSTRALIS

The Southern Right Whale is a baleen whale. Its stocky and fat body is black, with occasional white markings along the back and underside. It has no dorsal fin or any ridge along the back. The Southern Right Whales float higher on the water than other species of whales. They can grow to a length of 14 to 18 metres, and weigh on average about 41000 kg. Their cruising speed is 2 to 3 knots. After a gestation of about twelve months one calf is born, measuring 5 to 6 metres at birth.

The whale was judged 'right' to catch as it was rich in oil and floated easily after having been harpooned, hence its peculiar name. This slow-moving giant of the sea became one of the most ruthlessly hunted of all whale species. Since international protection (1935) the population has show consistent increases. The whale inhabits sub-antarctic waters between 30 degrees and 55 degrees south. They migrate south during the summer months when supplies of krill are more prolific, and north during winter and spring to mate, calve and rear their young.

It can be distinguished easily by its V-shaped 'blow' and the callosities for barnacles. Although barnacles and other sea life live on these patches on the whale's head, the callosities are actual outgrowths of tough skin which form different patterns on each individual - a useful form of identification. The 'blow' is a cloud of vapour produced largely by condensation when warm breath comes into contact with cooler air. It also contains oily mucous from the respiratory tract of the whale.

Whales are large brained and sensitive creatures. Strong bonds exist between females and their calves. They are normally non-aggressive and gentle.

Almost near the bottom of the road, as it bends fairly sharply to the left, use your imagination to spot a **'petrified'** family of **rock elephants**, bathing in the ocean, their trunks in the water, and the two youngest turning their head nosily.

The mountains shadowing the route, densely covered in vegetation, tumble steeply to the sea. Soon you are at **MILLER'S POINT**. Once the property of one Edmund Miller who, until 1850 conducted whaling operations in False Bay, it is now a pleasing coastal resort with playgrounds, a large tidal pool and picnic spots. The nearby **Black Marlin Restaurant** is reached on the same turn-off road as the resort.

En route to Simon's Town, you pass Murdock Valley, Oatlands and Froggy Farm.

But no doubt you want to see the famous **PENGUIN COLONY**? Famous, as it is unusual for penguins to breed on the mainland.

Continue past the windswept golf course on your right. The site was once a holding camp for Boer prisoners of war during the South African War 1899-1902. Watch out for a brown road sign on the left side of the road, marked **BOULDERS BEACH** and **PENGUINS**, immediately after the golf course.

Turn sharply right into Bellevue Road, drive to the parking area, and take the short walk to the beach.

Hundreds of **AFRICAN PENGUINS** frolic in the water, hop from boulder to boulder or waddle clumsily across the sand. Boulders Park is administered by the National Parks Board and an entrance fee is payable.

(Should you have missed the turn-off at the golf course, do not panic. Continue towards Seaforth and turn right into Seaforth Road. A short walk takes you to a viewing platform.)

The penguin colony established itself in the 1970's after an oil disaster.

The attractive black-white feathered African Penguin is an endangered species. Ashore the bird moves about rather awkwardly, but once in its watery element, the penguin shows off its prowess as a first class diver and agile swimmer.

The African Penguin is endemic to the south-western coast of southern Africa. They breed on 24 offshore islands between Namibia and Port Elizabeth. The colony at Boulders has found for itself an unusual, even dangerous breeding place, as breeding birds can readily fall prey to predators, including man.

Before the discovery of the suitability of guano in the manufacture of fertilisers, the African Penguin dug its nest sometimes several metres deep into guano. Since the commercial exploitation of guano which started in the 19th century, the penguins were forced to nest in sand or under protective ledges.

They breed throughout the year, laying normally two eggs. Adult birds feed during the day, whilst the chicks have to wait for their meal of re-gurgitated fish until the late afternoon. Usually the parents take turns in their duties: every 24 hours one of them guards the nest and the other swims out in search for food. They cover enormous distances hunting for food, up to 45 km at a speed of about 24km/h.! Sardines, anchovies, even squid make up their favourite meals.

Presently the total penguin population numbers about 160000 birds, a reduction, since 1930, of nearly 90%, when close to 1,2 million were counted. This figure dwindled in the mid 1950's to about 500000, and then plummeted in the late 1970's to a mere 230000. The bird falls prey to its natural preditors, man's exploitation of its breeding grounds and continuing oil pollution.

The birds are not quite as defenceless as they appear: they can inflict a very severe bite. Keep your distance. Do not agitate them by running or waving hands.

After this enthralling experience, you may be reluctant to return to your car. But the onward journey is equally fascinating as you approach **SIMON'S TOWN**.

Simon's Town street

The lively small coastal town was once known as **Isselsteijn** Bay named after a Dutch East Indiamen which sought shelter from strong winds in the Bay. Today it bears the name of Governor **Simon van der Stel** who explored the area in 1678, searching for safe winter anchorage. The Company's vessels in Table Bay fell all too often victim to unrelenting nor'westerly winter storms.

However, its distance from Cape Town and the difficulties in reaching it on an sometimes perilous overland route impeded the town's development until 1737. Only another catastrophic shipping disaster jolted the Dutch East India Company finally into action: nine ships in Table Bay, richly laden and ready to sail for the Netherlands were whipped once again by a savage storm. Seven ships beached near Salt River, broken up by the pounding of the ferocious seas...two hundred and eighty men drowned! This horrific disaster moved the lethargic Company to decide, four years later in 1741, that fleets should replenish themselves at Simon's Bay. Under the direction of **Baron van Imhoff** the port was officially opened in 1743.

At the time, the bay had already attracted one adventurous settler, **Antoni Visser**. In 1735 Visser had cared for the crew of the ill-fated vessel 'Texel' which impetuous seas had driven into False Bay. Thirty seven of her crew had already succumbed to sickness, another seventy five lay ill and only a handful remained able to look after the ailing crew members and the ship. Visser's home stood probably on the site of the present-day Admiralty

In the second half of the 18th century, under the austere but benevolent rule of **Governor Tulbagh**, additional buildings, such as a hospital, storehouse, slaughterhouse, bakery, workshops for smiths and other artisans and a house for the officer-in-charge were completed. In 1768 a stone pier with wooden piles was built.

Yet despite the unquestionable advantages of the bay, the Dutch Trading Company, financially on unsound footing, failed to develop its potential.

Again, external factors were forcing change upon the Cape.

In 1775, thousands of miles away, the colonists in the New World rebelled against England, refusing to submit to the Navigation Laws imposed on them in the middle of the 17th century. News of the successful rebellion also reached the ears of the burghers in the Cape. Hundreds signed a petition demanding the abolition of all private trade by officials of the Company, the granting of free trade with Holland, the Dutch Indies and ships from other nations. They also sought an increase in the price of wine, a lowering in farm rentals and permission to mete out corporal punishment to slaves without having to obtain prior permission to do so from the fiscal. The Company could ill afford to ignore these demands, but its hands were tied by the open warfare which had erupted in Europe as a direct result of the **American War of Independence**. France, Holland and Spain declared war on England, a war which was to greatly influence the fortunes of the Company at the Cape.

Britain, fearing for her Indian possession and a possible French capture of the Cape, dispatched a fleet, under **Commander Johnstone**, to wrest the Cape from the Dutch. Near the Cape Verde islands, the French and English fleets clashed. The naval battle at **Porto Prayo** left neither side victorious, and the French fleet, under Admiral de Suffren raced off to the Cape, reaching it before the British. The French stayed till 1784.

The French troops breathed some excitement into the economic and social life at the Cape, soon known as 'Little Paris'. The economic upswing was short-lived, however. The Company's obligation as an ally of France, to pay for expenses incurred by the French troops plunged it even deeper into debt and closer to the brink of financial ruin. In 1782 it paid its last dividend.

A VISITOR'S COMMENT ON LIFE AT THE CAPE

Bernardin de ST. PIERRE, author of the famous play 'Paul et Virginie', visited the Cape towards the end of the 18th century. He had this to say:
"When a man has seen one Dutch town, he has seen them all: it is the same here - the order of each house is alike. The custom of Madame Neethlin's was this: there was always company in the parlour, and a table covered with peaches, melons, apricots, raisins, pears, cheese, fresh butter, wine pipes and tobacco. At 8 o'clock they have a supper, as plentiful as their dinner. These good people are eating from morning to night."

Of the people in general he writes:
"They do not game, nor do they visit much. This people, content with domestic happiness, -the sure consequence of a virtuous life, do not yet seek after it in romances or upon the theatre. There are no public exhibitions at the cape, nor are they wished for. In his own house each man views the most pleasing, the most affecting of all spectacles - servants happy, children well brought up, and wives faithful and affectionate. They are a pensive set of people who choose rather to feel than to converse or to argue. Perhaps the want of subject is the case of their 'Taciturnity'."

When Britain recognised the independence of her American colonies, the threat to the Cape was over and in 1784 the French departed, plunging the dispirited burghers into a certain despondency as no concessions had yet been granted by the Company to their own demands.

Soon afterwards, the outbreak of the **French Revolution** in 1789 lit the flame of the revolutionary spirit, and plunged the European countries into war.

The Commissioner at the Cape, **Abraham Sluysken**, aware of Cape Town's vulnerability, erected Batteries at Camps Bay, Hout Bay and in Simon's Bay, armed with heavy guns.

As Amsterdam fell to the French in 1795 and the **Prince of Orange** fled to England, an alliance between Holland and France was formed. Britain was more than just willing to support the Prince of Orange's request to safeguard the Cape.

In June 1795 the British under Admiral Sir Keith Elphinstone and Major-General J.H. Craig, sailed into False Bay, fully expecting the Dutch authorities to submit to British protection. Sluysken, however, opted to play for time, eagerly awaiting news from Holland.

The situation for **Elphinstone** and **Craig** was equally unenviable. Not only were they bound to carry out their orders, but Sluysken's play for time could also lead to food and water shortages for their men. This potentially dangerous situation had to be averted and they determined to secure a foothold at Muizenberg, hoping to persevere with their negotiations from there.

View from Simon's Town towards Muizenberg

A narrow road linked Simon's Bay to Muizenberg, guarded by artillerymen, burgher cavalry and mercenaries. The British landed soldiers at Simon's Bay, and a column marched off towards Muizenberg. Meanwhile four ships, the *America*, *Stately*, *Rattlesnake* and the *Echo* raced across the Bay and anchored broadside to the Dutch camps at Muizenberg. When the British opened fire from the ships, the mercenaries, commanded by Colonel de Lille, fled. Then the burghers spotted the British column charging along the road. The outnumbered defenders, were driven back, but stood their ground. **Colonel de Lille** retreated to Wynberg. An indecisive battle was fought on the sandy stretches between Muizenberg and Wynberg. The odds against Sluysken, however, were mounting. His defensive strength had dwindled drastically. But, with spirits high, a company of burghers successfully overran the British near Steenberg, only to be finally driven off in a counter-attack.

General Craig, facing such unforseen and fierce defence, feared for his own position at Muizenberg. Then, finally, news broke that General Clarke had arrived in Simon's Bay with 14 ships, strengthening the British forces by a further 3000 troops.

Against such overwhelming odds Dutch resistance was powerless. The capitulation was signed on 16 September **1795** at Rustenburg, Rondebosch, marking the start of the **First British Occupation**.

Shortly after the capitulation, Sluijsken returned to Holland, whilst Clarke and Elphinstone sailed for India, leaving Major-General Craig and 3000 men behind at the Cape.

For seven years, until **1802**, the British governed the Cape, when in terms of the **Treaty of Amiens** it was returned to Holland then known as the Batavian Republic.

During these years, the financially ailing Dutch East India Company had finally collapsed in 1798.

By 1803 the military ambitions of Napoleon plunged Europe once again into war. France, allied with Spain and the Batavian Republic, challenged British power over the oceans. In 1805 news reached Simon's Bay that **Admiral Nelson** had crushed the combined fleets of France and Spain off Cape Trafalgar.

Despite her mastery of the seas, Britain continued to fear for her possessions in India: too many French warships were still at sea which could pose a threat to her growing empire. Possession of the strategic Cape was now of foremost importance. Thus, Britain dispatched a large fleet under the command of **Sir Home Popham**. Nearly 7000 soldiers, led by **General Baird**, landed at Bloubergstrand in January 1806. The men, who possessed first hand knowledge of the Cape from Britain's first occupation, totally outnumbered General Janssen's force. Resistance seemed pointless and Janssen, facing overwhelming odds, withdrew his men to Hottentots Holland, whilst **Colonel von Proplahow** surrendered Cape Town. The capitulation was signed at **Papendorf** (Woodstock) on **10 January 1806**.

Once more the British flag was raised over the Cape which the **Peace of Paris** finally declared a British possession in **1814**.

In 1814, Simon's Bay was declared the sole naval station at the Cape for the South Atlantic Squadron and a harbour constructed.

Simon's Town nestling at the foot of the Swartkop (678m) and Simonsberg (547) was ceded to the Admirality in 1895 as a naval station. It remained British territory until 2 April 1957, when the South African Navy took over the naval base. During and after the Boer War (1899 - 1902) extensive alterations were made to the harbour: new docks were built, a dry dock installed and numerous workshops added. During both World Wars, the town played a key role, more than 300 damaged ships were repaired here during World War II.

On the way to the town centre, you pass on the left the **OLD BURIAL GROUND**, dating back to 1813. This is one of the oldest cemeteries in the country.

A massive rock wall to the right shields the East Dockyard from curious passers-by. Within the naval docks the **MARTELLO TOWER** is of significance. Unfortunately it is not visible from the road.

MARTELLO TOWER, in the eastern dockyard, dates back to 1795. It was built by the British who, after capturing the Cape, wished to prevent possible attempts by Napoleon to occupy it. The original 'Martella' tower on the island of Corsica, at Cape Mortella, had been built to guard St. Fiorenzo Bay. In 1794 the British attacked this bay with two heavily armed warships, only to be repelled by fierce firing from the tower, manned by only 22 soldiers. Only a land attack eventually subdued the island. The British, deeply impressed by the strength of the building, built a similar tower in Simon's Town, changing the name to 'Martello'.

The gates to the East Dockyard which was officially opened in 1910 by HRH the Duke of Connaught, son of Queen Victoria, are rarely used today.

Take some time and stroll through the town, walking in a northerly direction towards the town centre.

On the hillside stands the Roman Catholic Church of **ST. SIMON AND ST. JUDE**, dating back to 1850.

The first Roman Catholic Bishop arrived in 1838 in the Cape. From then onward a priest was sent regularly to Simon's Town to minister to navy personnel. Services were conducted in military barracks, but the growing congregation needed a permanent place of worship. A chapel was built which again by 1885 had become too small. A new church, incorporating the old chapel was built on the hill.

You pass the white-washed **DUTCH REFORMED CHURCH**, built in 1856.

Once in Church Street, visit the **STEMPASTORI**. Here, in one of the rooms of the former manse, Dominee de Villiers composed in 1921 the music of the previous national anthem, Die Stem' ('The Voice of South Africa') replaced by 'Nkosi sikelele Afrika' ('God bless Africa) after the first democratic elections in 1994. In the other rooms replicas of the arms of various parts of South Africa and flags are exhibited.

Again, on the mountainside opposite the church, the buildings of the former Simon's Town Secondary School can be seen, which from 1950 housed the municipality. Presently the Simon's Town Administration is housed there.

Dutch Reformed Church

Still on the hillside, you find **THE OLD HOSPITAL TERRACE**. This was the old Royal Navy Hospital, built in 1813. It served as an hospital until 1902. Today it is home to senior naval officers.

THE WARRIOR TOY MUSEUM in St. George's Street is any child's dream world and adult's land of nostalgia with its fascinating exhibition of thousands of model cars, boats, trains, lead soldiers and a wide range of other toys.

The palms on **JUBILEE SQUARE**, named in honour of King George V. in 1935, lend a little welcome shade. They were planted in 1935, by a number of missionary schools and other institutions whose names are commemorated on a plaque on the Square. Before browsing in the boutiques or bartering with the loquacious hawkers, look at the bronze statue of a well-loved dog: **JUST NUISANCE**.

'Just Nuisance', a homeless Great Dane befriended the sailors during the Second World War. 'Able Seaman Just Nuisance' volunteered his services to the British Navy in August 1939 and was posted to the H.M.S. Afrikander, the Royal Navy's shore establishment. He even had his own bunk at Froggy Pond! As faithful companion to the young sailors, "Bonecrusher" would oversee their activities, accompany them on train trips to Cape Town and ensure they returned on time - keeping the young sailors out of trouble. He died, aged seven, and was buried with full military honours on 1 April 1944. Just Nuisance is an officer of the British Navy. His registration papers can be seen in the Simon's Town Museum.

Adjacent to the Square you find the 'Quarterdeck Restaurant' and the **Waterfront**, with its many curio, arts & crafts shops, the post office, restaurants and cafes, inviting you to rest a while and enjoy a tranquil view across the bay. Ships, yachts... the sea is calling!

Browse around in the many shops across the road as well. Enticing curios, friendly restaurants, antiques and books are waiting to be discovered by you.

Simon's Town Harbour

On the mountain side of the road some of ornate building façades are reminiscent of the English presence in the town. Look at the **BRITISH HOTEL**. The demand for accommodation when the town was the base of the Royal Navy's South Atlantic Squadron was great. Officers would frequently be accompanied by their families for the duration of their posting.

British Hotel

In 1900 a young nurse, Mary Henrietta Kingsley was posted to the Cape to work in the Royal Navy Hospital, the Old Hospital Terrace. She took a room in the British Hotel. Tirelessly she tended to the wounded of the Anglo-Boer War (1899-1902) and the victims of an outbreak of typhoid. She too succumbed, after only ten weeks, to the disease and was buried at sea.

Dockyard Church

The high brick walls hide most of the dockyard. Yet the wrought-iron gates of the West Dockyard allow you a glimpse of naval activities. One of the gates is still an original going back to 1863, whilst the other was built in 1966.

A little further on, the Dockyard Wall lowers and you can see the West Dockyard Residences. Here stood the first Postholder's House, built by the Dutch East India Company in 1758. The was remodelled and enlarged by the British. A gateway allows access to the **NAVAL MUSEUM**. It is well worth a visit with its fascinating exhibits.

The clock tower you see in the dockyard, is that of the **DOCKYARD CHURCH**, also and more correctly known as **ST. GEORGE'S CHURCH**.

To understand the naming of the various Anglican churches in the town, one needs to go back to the year 1814. The first Anglican congregation of Simon's Town assembled in an old store, today's **Criterion** building in St. George's Street, which had been rebuilt by Hermann Schutte according to the designs of Louis Thibault. This became known as St. George's Church. A few years later, heavy rains forced the congregation to move out, as the ceiling threatened to collapse. Services were then held in the Dragoons' unused stables and finally, as from 1819 in the **sail loft**. Until 1831 worship was conducted here when alterations forced the congregation to share the premises of the Wesleyan Chapel, built in 1828, on the hill above the town.

Meanwhile fundraising campaigns, supported by the Governor's wife Lady Francis Cole, raised sufficient money for the construction of a new Anglican

Church, the present **ST. FRANCIS CHURCH**, situated just outside the dockyards, next to the Simon's Town Museum.

In 1851 the spiritual welfare of the sailors was entrusted to a Naval Chaplain. Once again the sail loft resounded to the vigorous singing of worshippers on Sundays, but reverted to a much humbler rôle on weekdays when it was used for sailmaking! The altar was simply curtained off and the pews pushed against the wall. This arrangement lasted until 1935 when the sailmakers after completion of the repairs to the quarterdeck awning of the H.M.S. Dorsetshire, finally vacated that part of the loft which became the H.M. Dockyard Church - St. George's.

Worship demanded a certain degree of agility, as initially a narrow spiral staircase led to the entrance door, so narrow that only a person at a time could climb up! Imagine the dilemma when, in 1928, the first wedding was to be solemnised in this church. Ingeniously the problem was solved: a ladder was erected from the yard to the main hatch window so that bride and groom could stand side by side!

Today, stinkwood doors, on ground level, allow an easier and more elegant entry.

THE AERIAL ROPEWAY opposite the Dockyard Church was built by the Royal Navy in 1903/4. Today only pylons remain. It was used to transport sick sailors and goods from the docks to the Naval Hospital on the hill. The journey lasted about 15 minutes over a distance of 750m.

When you reach Court Road, turn right to visit the **OLD RESIDENCE/ SIMON'S TOWN MUSEUM**.

The **SIMON'S TOWN MUSEUM** is housed in the original **Residency**, built in the 1740's for the Governor's use. It is probably the oldest building in the town. It even boasts of its own ghost: that of 14-year old Eleanor MacCartney, daughter of Governor

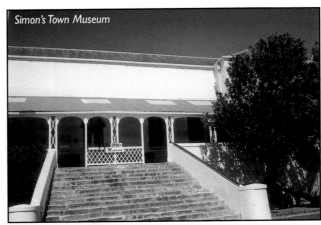

Simon's Town Museum

MacCartney. She died of pneumonia.

The museum exhibits valuable relics of the town's past. One section is devoted to the famous dog, Just Nuisance.

Admiralty

The grounds of the **ADMIRALTY** stretch from the corner of Court Road and St. George's Street northwards.

The **ADMIRALTY BUILDING** stands on the land once granted to probably the town's first inhabitant, Antoni Visser. After his death, the property passed through many hands, until it was bought in 1785 by William Hurter. He opened a lodging house with about twenty rooms and this his widow carried on after his death. She eventually sold it to the navy and it became the official residence of the commander-in-chief.

Tired from strolling up and down the main street? Let's continue the journey now by car.

A couple of hundred metres after the Admiralty, look up to the left. The white-washed walls of the **PALACE BARRACKS** can be seen. Sadly the building, once an architectural jewel of the town, is in a poor state of repair.

One of the most distinguished characters of Simon's Town was John Osmond. As a ship's carpenter he arrived here in 1799, aboard the HMS Lancaster. Diligent and competent, he rose to the rank of master shipwright. He chose wisely when he married the daughter of a wealthy widow, and displayed equal business genius at the end of the First British occupation when he established a ship-repairing business. Together with his mother-in-law, Osmond purchased a number of

HORATIO NELSON

in Simon's Bay. In 1774 the young midshipman, Horatio Nelson, arrived at the Cape, en route for Madras. Only two years later, the frigate HMS Dolphin anchored in Simon's Bay with the young Nelson seriously ill on board. He was being invalided home. Though the ship stayed for nearly a month, Horatio Nelson never came ashore.

properties. For himself he chose an elegant home 'Mount Curtis', said to be second only to Admiralty House in stateliness. Soon he became known as King John, while his home was spoken of as the 'Palace' (later to become the Palace Barracks). Like many others, he profited from Napoleon's presence on St. Helena.

In modern times the Palace Barracks served as the Petty Officers and Warrant Officers Mess, today it is waiting for new occupants.

FROM SIMON'S TOWN TO GROOT CONSTANTIA

Just outside the town lies the station, on the right. Simon's Town is the terminus of the suburban railway line from Cape Town, built towards the end of the 19th century. The train ride which hugs the coast from Simon's Town to Muizenberg, lasts just over an hour.

Looking out across False Bay you see **ROMAN ROCK LIGHTHOUSE**, the third oldest in the country, and the only one built on a rock. The rock is visible at low tide. The lighthouse stands 17 m high. It was commissioned after four years of construction in 1861. The present light, with a moving rotating optic, was installed in 1992 and its intensity increased to 147 000 CD and a range of 20 nautical miles.

Driving on, the Redhill Road (M 66), joins on the left. Ignore this turn-off, as it leads back across the mountains towards the Atlantic Ocean. Continue to Dido Valley. Turn left and visit the **Mineral World**. Here semi-precious stones are washed, tumbled, sorted, set and crafted into attractive objects of art and jewellery. The shop offers a wonderful selection and for those who feel like 'discovering' their own stones, the 'Scratch Patch' where thousands of stones are strewn across a sand pit, offers an ideal opportunity.

Out in the surf, the tops of the triple expansion cylinders of the steam ship **'SS Clan Stuart'** are visible. This 3594-ton coaler became a victim of a southeasterly gale and went ashore at Glencairn in 1914. The crew was saved.

Now you have reached **GLENCAIRN**. It owes its name to a bagpipe playing Scotchman who originated from the real Glencairn in Scotland.

Glencairn enjoyed a brief spell of fame when in 1902 the first glass manufacturing factory started production here. The Cape Glass Company Ltd had been established by the Norwegian founder of Ohlsson's Brewery in 1902. It was probably the first glass factory in the southern hemisphere that produced glass bottles by machine. Every 24 hours 10 000 bottles were manufactured. Unfortunately the factory was considered a failure and ceased production in 1905.

A small river, the Else Rivier traverses the Glencairn Valley, dominated by the 228m high **Elsies Peak**.

Ou Kaapse Weg winding through Silvermine

To the left, the M4 is joined by the GLENCAIRN EXPRESSWAY. This route would lead back towards the M65 (Kommetjie Road) and on to OU KAAPSE WEG (M 64) a scenic route over the Silvermine Mountains. Ultimately it will link up with the route which is being followed in this guide now.

Shortly you come to the small coastal town of **FISH HOEK** which, until the mid 1990's was the only absolutely 'dry' town of the country. The prohibition of the sale of alcohol dates back to the early nineteenth century when Governor Lord Charles Somerset stipulated in the title deed granted to Albertus Bruins that *"no public wine houses"* were to be built on the land.

The town's name appears on maps as early as 1725, but it was not settled until 1818.

Fish Hoek nestles in a sandy glen which cuts right across the southern peninsula. Many thousand years ago, the sea washed through this valley, leaving behind the present sandy floor. In pre-historic times, man must have lived here. Skeleton finds in 1927 in a rock shelter then known as *Schildersgat* (Painter's Cave) point to this fact. The discovery was made by the father and son team Victor and Bertram Peers. The skeleton, known as 'Fish Hoek Man' ante-dates Neanderthal. The cave is known today as **'Peer's Cave'**.

Fish Hoek

Stay on the M4 which takes you through the busy town's centre: at the traffic isle and junction with the M65, signposted 'Kommetjie', bear right.

Soon you pass through **CLOVELLY** where the Silvermine Stream reaches the sea. This area was once a farm named *'Klein Tuin'* (Little Garden).

Continue to **KALK BAY** - The Lime Bay, where many years ago a busy kiln produced lime for painting buildings, giving the town its name.

*At the traffic lights opposite the harbour entrance, you must decide whether to stay on the main road leading you through Kalk Bay on to St. James and Muizenberg, **OR** whether to turn left into Clairvaux Road and follow Boyes Drive:*

Boyes Drive, about 100 metres above the sea, presents magnificent views of the picturesque Kalk Bay fishing harbour, St James, Muizenberg, Sandvlei, Marina da Gama and False Bay. There are numerous parking facilities along the road for you to pause and marvel at the stunning views. Be careful of fast moving traffic when you cross Boyes Drive.

The Boyes Drive route leads to Lakeside.

The coastal main road option allows you to explore Kalk Bay, its antique shops, and the interesting architecture of Muizenberg.

Kalk Bay Harbour

But stroll also through the colourful, lively harbour. It is always active, particularly during the snoek season. The sharp toothed SNOEK, a local, much loved delicacy, is a barracuda-like fish weighing up to nine kilogram.

The first train steamed into KALK BAY in May 1883. Laying the tracks along the sandy, stormy shores had proved to be a monumental task. Many locals had welcomed the advent of easier travel, but Kalk Bay's fishermen vehemently rejected the proposal that the line was to go across a viaduct spanning the beach. A viaduct would cut off access to the beach and thwart attempts to pull their their boats to safety in high spring tides and stormy weather. Thus, alternative routes

Snoek for sale!

along the mountain side were investigated, but the cost of construction found to be prohibitively high. In the end, the viaduct was built. A few years later, as if to vindicate the fishermen's protest, a violent storm smashed 17 boats. The fishermen failed to pull them to safety across the road, as had been the custom, out of reach of the ferocious waves.

For better shelter, the fishermen agitated, successfully, for the construction of a breakwater: the foundation stone was laid in 1913.

Incidentally, large scale commercial netting in the bay was forbidden in 1983.

Rising above Kalk Bay and serenely overlooking False Bay are the **Kalk Bay Mountains**, famed for their splendid fynbos vegetation, scenic walks, and many numerous caves. One of them, the **Boomslang Cave** penetrates a ridge of 146 metres.

The road now leads through **ST. JAMES**, a small seaside resort takes its name from the first church built here by Roman Catholics in 1852. Unfortunately it fell victim to progress as its site was needed for the construction of the railway station. The priest agreed to an exchange of place on condition that the new station be named "St. James".

Soon you have reached **MUIZENBERG** which developed from a humble cattle outpost for the Dutch East India Company, but assumed a more active

Muizenberg beach

rôle as a military post after 1743 when Simon's Town had become an official anchorage. It is named after the soldier Muijs who guarded the Company's cattle outpost here. Fishermen had always been lured to its splendid coastline, as were the whalers in the early twentieth century.

Growth accelerated after 1882, when the railway line had reached Muizenberg.

Mining magnates, prominent business men and politicians such as Cecil John Rhodes, Prime Minister of the Cape towards the end of the 19th century, purchased properties here. Muizenberg rose in prominence, acquiring an aura of prestige which tempted even the writer and poet Rudyard Kipling (a friend of Rhodes) and Agatha Christie to spend their holidays here.

A much loved halfway-house in the 1920's was Farmer Peck's Inn, a name echoed today only by one of the mountain ravines overlooking the town.

Take the opportunity and visit the small **thatched cottage, last home of Cecil John Rhodes**, on the left of the main road.

CECIL JOHN RHODES

Cecil John Rhodes landed in the Cape in 1870. He was a sickly young man, suffering from tuberculosis. He joined his brother Herbert, who farmed cotton, hoping to find a cure for his ailment. The peaceful farmlife was shattered within a year of his arrival by the news of the discovery of diamonds. The Rhodes brothers abandoned their farm, joined the rush to Griqualand West where they established three claims. Luck was on their side, they prospered, but then tragedy struck when Herbert was burned to death on a camping trip.

Undeterred, young Cecil continued and in 1880, he formed the DE BEERS Mining Company. His greatest rival, Barny Barnato, was bought out for a sum of over £ 5 million.

Despite his business affairs demanding his concentration, Rhodes returned to his studies in Oxford, fighting off many a health crisis which badly weakened his heart and lungs. He expanded his empire in 1887 when he founded the GOLD FIELDS of SA Company. By 1893 his 'British South Africa Company' was a major force in the economy of the then Rhodesia. (Zimbabwe) His influence as parliamentarian was equally strong. In 1881 he became a member of Parliament for Barkly West and finally Prime Minister of the Cape in 1890. He dreamt of a South African Federation within the British Empire. In an attempt to overthrow President Kruger and gain supreme power, Rhodes supported the ill fated Jameson Raid from Rhodesia (Zimbabwe) into the Transvaal.

The raiders, led by Sir Leander Starr Jameson were utterly routed and Rhodes forced to relinquish his premiership in 1896. In the same year he quelled an uprising of the Ndebele, directed the construction of a bridge over the Zambesi at Victoria Falls, launched the Rhodes Fruit Farms in the Cape, and drew up a will that ploughed back into Southern Africa much of the fortune he had made. He died in March 1902. His body was taken by train to the Matopos Hills in Zimbabwe, a country that once bore his name 'Rhodesia'.

RHODES COTTAGE was built in the 1870's. Rhodes, who died here in March 1902, bought it in 1899 from the estate of John Robertson Reid. The original thatch roof had been replaced by corrugated iron when Rhodes owned it. After his return from England in 1902, he drove down to the cottage in his 12-14hp

Wolseley car he had brought with him from England. He was already suffering from the heart disease which was to cause his death. Exhausted from the trip down to the coast, Rhodes retired to bed, propped up by pillows to ease his difficulty in breathing, aggravated by the extremely hot weather conditions. Finally, to allow some air to penetrate, a hole was made in the iron roof. The cottage was proclaimed a National Monument in 1938.

After your visit to the Cottage, tucked behind a high hedge, again look left.

You pass the **SOUTH AFRICAN POLICE MUSEUM** complex. It consists of the old Police Station and the Court, the former post office. (This post office had been the first to receive mail by air in South Africa in 1911). The museum exhibits uniforms, numerous police items and antique furniture.

Posthuys

A quaint, white-washed building comes into view: the **POSTHUYS**. Built in 1673, the Posthuys is the oldest structure in the country, as it ante-dates the completion of the Castle. It served at first as a look-out post for the Dutch East India Company, then after 1806, as the Commandant's Quarters for the British troop commander in Muizenberg and finally, towards the end of the 19th century, it was turned into a holiday cottage. It was restored in 1982/3 by the Anglo American Corporation.

Labia residence

Contrasting sharply with the unassuming Posthuys is an imposing building, again on the left side of the road: the grandiose Venetian-styled former residence of **Prince Natale Labia**, once Italy's diplomatic representative to South Africa. It was built in 1929/30 on the site of an old British military battery. The interior fittings were imported from Venice. Prince Labia died in 1936. After the death of his wife, Countess Labia in 1961, the family donated the property to the State and it opened as the **NATALE LABIA MUSEUM** (NM) in 1988. As a satellite gallery of the SA National Gallery, it houses fine works of art.

Look across the road and you can not fail to be impressed by the striking architecture of the **STATION BUILDING**, with its intriguing tower. Built in red brick in 1912-13 with sandstone rustication, it is a fine example of the Edwardian era.

(To reach the beaches, turn right into Atlantic/Beach Roads at the traffic lights.)

Muizenberg Station

The M4 then passes through Lakeside, Zandvlei. Across the *'vlei'* (lake), the whitewashed houses of Marina da Gama nestle on the water's edge.

The *vleis* close to the shores of False Bay are fed by numerous streams, like the *Spaansemat* (Spanish Rushes) and the *Diep Rivier* (Deep River). Tumbling down from the nearby mountains, the rivers soon reach the level ground of the Cape Flats. Here, depressions in the former sandy sea bed catch some of the water, slowing the flow and forming shallow lakelets such as Zandvlei, which is fed by the Spaansemat Rivier. The vlei is popular with canoeists and boardsailors.

Just outside Lakeside, the M4 is joined by Boyes Drive. Continue straight for a few hundred metres, then turn left (M42)at the traffic lights.

If you are in a rush select the RIGHT LANE to filter into the M3 Simon van der Stel Freeway. Follow the M3 all the way back to Cape Town, allowing for a turn-off to Kirstenbosch. (signposted)

But for the more scenic route, stay in the LEFT LANE. The M42 goes past **Steenberg Estate** - where a little winetasting can be enjoyed - towards **Tokai**. The name echoes the Tokai Hills in Hungary, home of a delicious wine of the same name. Cool pine forests shade the route. The Tokai Forest was established in the early 1880's, when re-afforestation was the official policy for the area. A large experimental nursery was established, South Africa's first arboretum.

You pass **Pollsmoor Prison**, on your right, where **Nelson Mandela** also spent some time as political prisoner, before his transfer to a prison in Paarl.

NELSON MANDELA

NELSON MANDELA was born into the royal Thembu family in 1918, near Umtata. His involvement in student politics at Fort Hare University resulted in his expulsion from the university. Mandela was an active member of the ANC Youth League in the late 1940s, early 1950s and became increasingly involved in organising Congress resistance to government policies. In 1952 he and Oliver Tambo opened the first black law practice in the country. In 1961 he was acquitted on charges of treason. After the Sharpeville massacres, he was instrumental in the formation of the ANC's military wing, Umkhonto we Sizwe ('The Spear of the Nation')and was its first commander-in-chief. Mandela was re-arrested in 1962, and in the Rivonia Trial sentenced to life imprisonment in 1964, on charges of sabotage and planning guerrilla warfare. He was incarcerated for 27 years as political prisoner, and finally released on 11 February 1990.

THE AFRICAN NATIONAL CONGRESS (ANC)

The ANC was formed in 1912. The Act of Union (1910) had curtailed African political rights; a group of black influential professionals in Bloemfontein formed the South African Native National Congress. Its delegations sent to Cape Town and London failed to prevent the introduction of segregationist laws, in 1914 and 1919. In 1923 the Congress adopted the name African National Congress. Up to the end of the 1930s, the ANC remained a small organisation, leaving mass mobilisation to the Industrial and Commercial Workers Union and the Communist Party. Only during the war years the ANC turned into a mass organisation. The Youth League, of which Mandela was a founder member, was set up at Fort Hare in 1944. Its aim was to steer the ANC towards a more militant black nationalism, pride in black culture and race. In 1956, The ANC adopted the Freedom Charter which confirmed that South Africa belonged to all its inhabitants, black and white. It called for a non-racial, democratic system of government, equality before the law, equal work and educational opportunities, nationalisation of banks, mines and heavy industry and the redistribution of land. Four years later, in 1960, the ANC was banned. A two year sabotage campaign orchestrated by Umkhonto started in 1961: the first bombs exploded. The ANC resumed guerrilla warfare in 1977, but as such the ANC's activities were directed from exile. During this period closer links were forged with the Communist Party. The first non-black members were admitted to the ANC at the Morogoro Conference in 1969. By the end of 1980s, economic recession and political stalemate prompted the South African government to legalise the ANC.

As you approach the junction with Tokai Road, turn left if you wish to see (but you can not enter) the old **TOKAI MANOR HOUSE** at the end of Tokai Road.

This picturesque house is situated on the lower slopes of the Constantiaberg Mountain, on a portion of Simon van der Stel's former grazing lands. It is a national monument.

The land was first granted in 1792 to a Johan Andreas Rauch, head of the armoury. Within two months of the grant, he sold the land to Andries Teubes. The latter probably built the homestead in 1795-96, according to a design by Louis Thibault, a renowned French architect. Characteristics of his design are the high *stoep* (terrace), the round pillars and the raised artificial freestone. The farm changed hands several times before it became the property of Petrus Eksteen in 1802. It remained in the Eksteen family until 1882 when the Government acquired the property and developed a forest nursery.

The route (M42) crosses the verdant Constantia valley, changing name from Orpen Road to Spaansemat Road. At the intersection with Ladies Mile Rd, turn left into Ladies Mile Extension, until you reach the traffic lights at the intersection with the M41,(Main Road). The road sign directs you quite clearly to the left for Groot Constantia. Follow the route until you reach the signposted turn-off to the left to **GROOT CONSTANTIA**.

Towards the end of the seventeenth century, governor **Simon van der Stel** was granted 762 hectares of land by Baron van Rheede, a high ranking official of the Dutch East India Company. Grateful for this magnanimous gesture, the governor named the land after the baron's young daughter *'Constantia'*. His unofficial residence (the Governor's official residence was in the Castle) soon became a focal point of social engagements, popular soirées, as Simon van der Stel enjoyed a reputation as a man of taste, intelligence and culture. At the end of his term as governor, Simon van der Stel retired to his beloved homestead where he died in 1712. The unfortunate removal of his successor, his son Willem, from office because of malpractices led eventually to the division of the magnificent farm. One part of the farm, including the main house, passed into the hands of one Oloff Bergh, once a trusted but later disowned employee of Simon van der Stel.

Another portion was sold to one Pieter de Meyer and named Bergvliet. In the course of time Bergvliet was sub-divided once more giving rise to the farms of Klein Constantia, Hoop of Constantia, Buitenverwachting,

Witteboomen, Silverhurst and others. After Bergh's death Groot Constantia passed successively to Carel Wieser, Jacobus van der Spuy and Jan Serrurier, before it became the property in 1778, of HENDRIK CLOETE.

Cloete engaged the services of the architect **Thibault** to rebuild the run-down house and a new wine cellar. As was so often the case with buildings in Cape Town, Thibault's design work was complemented by the creations of the German sculptor, **Anton Anreith**. He executed the **'Figure of Plenty'** in the niche of the front gable as well as the well-known pediment of the wine cellar, which stands directly behind the manor house. In this handsome pediment Ganymed, cup bearer to Zeus is shown astride on an eagle, an attribute of Zeus. He is flanked by bacchantes holding bunches of grapes, as well as by panthers who are an attribute of Bacchus; some of the bacchantes hold a drape in their plump little hands, and the background is formed by the outline of wine casks. The sculpture is made of lime plaster, the projecting masses being held by a brick core.

Cloete widened the front rooms of the main homestead and the adjoining hall. This necessitated the lifting of the roof, changing its pitch dramatically. Usually a thatch roof pitch remained at 50 degrees, because of a lack of lateral resistance of Cape walls. The new roof, as you will see, is pitched much steeper. The walls too were heightened by one metre, and the sash windows lengthened. After the heightening of the roof, the gable seemed much larger and barer, in fact a little lifeless. It was for this reason that Anreith was asked to create a suitable sculpture for it, the 'Figure of Plenty'.

The Cloete family left the estate amidst deadly outbreaks of a vine sickness Oidium and Phylloxera. So bad was the situation for them that they sold the estate to the Cape government for just over R 10 000 in 1885. But much worse was to come when a fire nearly destroyed the entire estate. In 1927 it was faithfully restored to its former glory by the architect F.K. Kendall.

Today, the homestead is in excellent condition. It exhibits furniture and ornaments of the period, donated largely by the shipping magnate **Alfred Aaron de Pass**. A management body was established to improve the estate in 1975. In 1993 through the establishment of the 'Groot Constantia Trust', the estate was released from state ownership which had begun in 1885.

Enjoy the tasty fare in either of the two restaurants, browse around the museum shop or taste a little wine.

THE STORY OF A GREAT WINE

Simon Van der Stel had planted the oak trees and about 70 000 vines on his estate, especially of the white muscadel variety, known also as the Muscat de Grontignon, the red Pontac, a red Muscadel and white Steen. When Hendrik Cloete took over the portion of the original estate of Groot Constantia, he planted 10 000 new vines. Cloete was related to Johannes Colyn, owner of one of the other portions of the farm after sub-division, known as De Hoop op Constantia. The two men produced on their estates what became two of the greatest wines in the world - the legendary white and red Constantia wines. Indeed, Red Constantia wines became so sought after in the cellars of Europe that King Louis Phillippe of France bought the entire vintage in 1833!

No description exists of the creating of these famous wines. Laboratory tests of a few surviving bottles discovered in such cellars as that of the Duke of Northumberland revealed an alcoholic content of 13,42 per cent in the red, 15,01 per cent in the white wine and a sugar content in both of about 128 grams per litre! The flavour resembled a delicious raisin-like liqueur. Frederick the Great of Prussia, the German Chancellor Bismarck, the kings of Holland, France and Britain: all of them cherished the Constantia wines. Even Napoleon found solace in it on St.Helena, drinking a bottle each day. He asked for a glass of it just before he died.

What happened to these famous wines?

When the estate became Cape Government property in 1885, wine production ceased for almost a hundred years. Then, in 1980, Constantia awoke from its slumber: Douglas Jooste bought the portion of the old estate known as Klein Constantia. Supported by a brilliant team of viticulturists and wine authorities, he set to work.

Remnants of vines planted by van der Stel were discovered, from which clones were produced. These were planted on Klein Constantia. Following the techniques of the old winemakers, the crop was carefully pruned and the remaining grapes left

STEPPE BUZZARD

Amazingly, even the Steppe Buzzard contributes to the excellence of Constantia wines. Each year in November, the buzzard migrates across Africa to escape the harsh Siberian winters. Until the end of March these raptors guard the vineyards, wheeling and coursing over the vines with their ripening grapes, thus chasing and often killing fruit-eating birds. By the time the buzzards migrate back to Siberia, the vines have been harvested and the wine is maturing in the casks.

to fully ripen. Late in March, when the grapes resembled shrivelled raisins and were sweet as honey, they were picked. In 1986 the young wine was put into wood for slow, leisurely maturation. Three years later, the first bottle was opened: the sweet, seductive *Vin de Constance* had returned.

SIMON VAN DER STEL

Who was this frequently mentioned Governor van der Stel?

A new era dawned for the settlers when Simon van der Stel assumed the office of governor in 1679. He lacked neither ambition, energy, willpower nor determination, characteristics which he inherited from his father Adrian, who had been governor of Ceylon (Sri Lanka) and Mauritius, and whose murder he had witnessed as a child. The young van der Stel returned to Holland where he enjoyed the best possible education at the time. His choice of study subjects which included agriculture, viticulture, horticulture and economics, appear to have prepared him well for his future rôle at the Cape.

Even his choice of wife seems premeditated. Was it love or cool calculation when he led Johanna Bax, daughter of a wealthy and influential Amsterdam family, patrons of Rembrandt, to the altar? The influence of his wife's family extended as far as the Cape, where a relative, Johann Bax van Heerental was governor at the time of his marriage. His wife bore him several children, and the couple appeared, on the surface, happy. But the marital bliss hardly stood up to closer scrutiny as the van der Stels were rarely seen together at official functions. And the seemingly impossible happened: Simon van der Stel sets sail, with his children, for Africa, leaving his wife behind! She bluntly refused to accompany him to this wild continent. His departure marks the end of their relationship as no letters found their way to or from Africa in the ensuing 30 years; the silence suggesting that this marriage was probably a means to an end, to have the official doors open for him.

Shortly after his arrival at the Cape, Simon van der Stel settled eight families in the valley of the Eerste River, a settlement today known as Stellenbosch.

FROM GROOT CONSTANTIA VIA KIRSTENBOSCH AND RHODES MEMORIAL TO THE CITY

It is time to bid farewell to Groot Constantia. Once you have passed through the entrance gates again, turn left, to rejoin the M41. The road snakes its way steadily uphill through the leafy Constantia valley until it reaches the traffic circle at **Constantia Nek**. To the left lies the Constantia Nek Restaurant. Swing half-way around the circle and join **Rhodes Avenue** (M63). This scenic route along the eastern foothills of Table Mountain with enviable views across to False Bay, past lavish private homes and resplendent gardens leads directly to Kirstenbosch National Botanical Gardens.

(Note, there are two entrances. The upper gate is situated directly opposite Klassens Road, where parking is available. For the lower entrance gate, continue on the M63 until you reach a traffic isle, bear left to reach the gates. It is clearly signposted!)

KIRSTENBOSCH NATIONAL BOTANICAL GARDENS nestles on the eastern slopes of Table Mountain, between an altitude of about 100 m above sea level at the lower gate and 1086 m at Maclears Beacon.

The northern slopes of the Gardens are characterised by underlying sedimentary shales and greywackes. The latter is a conglomerate rock of rounded pebbles and sand cemented together. Both shales and greywackes belong to the Malmesbury Group, which formed about 800 million years ago during the Precambrian period. In the southern part they make contact with an intrusion of igneous Cape granite.

The steep cliffs rising above the Gardens are part of the sedimentary Table Mountain Group which formed about 400 million years ago during the Paleozoic era. This group includes the Graafwater Formation, a relatively narrow band of maroon coloured shales and siltstones which are visible at the level of the 300m contour path, and the Peninsula Formation of light coloured quartzite sandstone which forms cliffs up to 600m.

On Wynberg Ridge as well as in the lower parts of Kirstenbosch a higher clay content enriches the soil which otherwise, is mostly sandy, with large deposits of scree.

A number of geological faults incise the mountain in this area, mostly corresponding to the position of gorges and streams such as Skeleton,

Nursery, Window and Hiddingh Ravines.

Historically, the eastern slopes of Table Mountain also played a significant rôle as it was here that Jan van Riebeeck, in 1657, handed out the first sawing rights by permitting Leenderts Cornelissen to collect timber. Three years later, van Riebeeck gave instructions to plant a hedge of wild almonds as a protection against 'Hottentot' raids. Remnants of the 'Van Riebeeck Hedge' can still be seen.

Until 1811, the ground of the present Gardens was state owned, when it was purchased by the Colonial Secretary and his Deputy, H. Alexander and Colonel Bird respectively. In later years it was owned by the Cloete and Eksteen families before being purchased, in 1895, by Cecil John Rhodes for £ 9000 as part of his intention to set aside the eastern reaches of Table Mountain as a public park. On his death in 1902, Rhodes bequeathed the property to the nation.

In 1911 it was selected as the site for a national botanical garden which was proclaimed in 1913. Its first director was Professor Harold Pearson. Under his directorship began the programme of education to encourage the growth and cultivation of indigenous flora.

The Garden covers some 528 hectares and includes both a cultivated section and a nature reserve, stretching as high up as **Maclear's Beacon**, the highest point of Table Mountain (1086m).

Take time to explore the floral wealth on display, stroll through the theme gardens - the **Fynbos Walk, Fragrance** and **Medicinal Gardens**, as well as the **water-wise garden** corner.

Maps and green-white direction pathfinders guide you through the Gardens. All along, information boards supply a background to the people, plants and historical development of Kirstenbosch. Many plants are labelled with details of the plant family, its scientific name, a common name, if available, and information about its natural distribution in southern Africa. At the bottom left hand corner of the label is an accession number which relates to information about the plant kept in the Kirstenbosch plant records. The last two numbers refer to the year in which the plant was introduced to Kirstenbosch National Botanical Gardens. In 1983, the plant records were computerised and all plants not previously recorded were given the reference number /83.

The **Conservatory** with over 4500 plant species in cultivation at the lower end of the Gardens will captivate you.

Guided walks through the Garden and the Conservatory can be arranged, whilst several trails lead through the natural forest and fynbos, ranging from 1,5 km to 7,8 km.

If you are fortunate enough to visit the Gardens in mid-summer, you may even enjoy the 'Summer Concerts' held on late Sunday afternoons. What a spectacular stage...

Walking the many paths at Kirstenbosch probably left you tired, thirsty and hungry. But the restaurant and coffee bar will energize you sufficiently to browse around in the shops.

But the tour continues! At the exit, turn left into the M63 (Rhodes Avenue). Continue to the traffic lights, turn left again into the M3, known as Union Drive, Rhodes Drive and finally the last section before reaching Cape Town, De Waal Drive.

The next visit is to the **RHODES MEMORIAL**.

The turn-off to the left, at the 'Princess Anne' interchange, is clearly signposted 'Rhodes Memorial'.

Follow the fairly narrow road through Groote Schuur Estate. Below lies the University of Cape Town. There is ample parking near the Memorial, as well as a cosy restaurant.

RHODES MEMORIAL, built in 1912, honours Cecil John Rhodes who loved this site on the lower slopes of 'Devil's Peak'. Here, in the stillness of the mountain, he could ponder, brood and dwell on his imperial dream of a British Empire from the Cape to Cairo. When he died in 1902, his friend the poet **Rudyard Kipling** wrote of him:

> *"The immense and brooding spirit still shall quicken and control.*
> *Living he was the land and dead his soul shall be her soul"*
>
> (words inscribed on a plaque underneath the bronze bust of Cecil John Rhodes at the Memorial)

Forty nine steps lead up to the memorial, designed, in granite, by **Sir Herbert Baker** and **Francis Masey**.

The powerful force that dominated Rhodes' life flows from the equestrian statue, **'Energy'** created by **G.F. Watts**.

The views from the Memorial across Cape Town are dazzling.

Return now the same way and turn left, to re-join the M3. Soon the first buildings and rugby fields of the **UNIVERSITY OF CAPE TOWN** can be seen on the left, against the striking backdrop of Devil's Peak, and the back of Table Mountain.

The University of Cape Town is the oldest university in the country, dating back to 1829. Then it was known as the South African College School which by 1841 was housed in the Egyptian Building, in the old Company's Garden in town. The college campus was moved to its present site in 1925, when the foundation stone for the first building was laid by the Prince of Wales. The university's impressive site on the Groote Schuur Estate is part of Cecil John Rhodes' bequest to the nation.

The present university campus stretches across De Waal Drive where many residences, administration buildings and the Faculties of Ballet and Music are situated.

Once past the ivy-clad walls look ahead towards the pedestrian bridge spanning the road. Perhaps you can make out already the wings of a famous historical landmark, the **MOSTERT MILL**?

The mill, an historical monument, stands on the former Welgelegen Farm and is of a type known in Holland as a 'boven-kruier' (over-shot) wheatmill. It was built in 1796 and named after Sybrand Mostert, a great-grandson of the Cape's first miller. Cecil John Rhodes purchased the farm in 1891 when the mill was no longer functional. It was extensively restored in 1936 and since then it is being maintained in working order.

Mostert Mill

The journey nears its end. As De Waal Drive curves gently uphill one last imposing building complex comes into view: **GROOTE SCHUUR HOSPITAL** ('The Big Barn')which earned world renown in 1967 when Professor Chris Barnard performed the first human heart transplant.

Look up to the slopes of **Devils Peak** (1000m), which owes its name to the legendary meeting between the devil and Van Hunk, the pirate who nearly lost his soul to the archfiend.

Perhaps you can just make out the ruins of an old fort?

The defence of Cape Town had long been a sore point, going back as far as the days of van Riebeeck when a gunner apparently ridiculed the siting of the new stone castle, as he believed it could easily be hit by guns from the slopes of Devil's Peak. The gunner was challenged to fire a shot, but prudently his shot fell short of the building site...

To secure the mountain the British built three blockhouses calling them **'King's'**, **'York'** (also known as **'Queen's'**) and **'Prince of Wales'**. They formed a triangle with the 'King's Blockhouse' standing at the apex high on the slopes of Devil's Peak, and the other two forming the base.

The 'King's Blockhouse' served as a convict station from 1893 to the 1920s when the afforestation work on Devil's Peak was carried out with convict labour.

The Prince of Wales Blockhouse was demolished in 1926. All that remains is a stone terrace and ruins of some buildings whilst the 'Queen's Blockhouse' although a mere ruin, has been allowed to stand as a silent reminder of the troubled times, under the wings of the Cape Town Historical Society.

Approaching Groote Schuur Hospital, choose your traffic lane! But be careful of frantic drivers whizzing past on either side, or just about taking off your bumper as they cut in front of you. Cape Town drivers all too often display a complete disregard for the rules of the road.

You can return to the city either via DE WAAL DRIVE (M3) or THE EASTERN BOULEVARD (N2). The view from either route sweeps from Table Mountain across to Table Bay, the harbour, the suburbs and the northern shores - and the city, comfortably nestling at the foot of Table Mountain, bids welcome once again!

Long before the first Europeans stepped ashore, the Khoi people grazed their sheep in the shade of **'Hoeri kwagga'**, meaning **'Sea Mountain'**. Would they have challenged the mountain and reach the top or would the Portuguese admiral, **Antonio da Saldanha**, have been the first in 1502? The admiral, unsure of the route ahead, ascended the steep Platteklip ('Flatstone') Gorge to get his bearings. Impressed by the mountain's seemingly flat top da Saldanha named it **'Taboa do Cabo'** - Table Mountain- a name it would never lose.

Platteklip Gorge, in years to come, was to offer shelter for runaway slaves. In 1797, it made headlines when the first woman to climb Table Mountain, Lady Ann Barnard, followed its narrow track to reach the top.

Its perennial stream, called the **'Verse Rivier'** ('Freshwater River') by the Dutch settlers, caused a refreshment station to be built here - Cape Town. Slaves would carry heavy loads of washing to the bubbling stream and then lay it out on the flat rocks to dry in the sun - hence Platteklip. During the last quarter of the 19th century, wash houses were built here with wash tubs and ironing facilities, which only closed in 1959/1960.

Table Mountain forms the northern boundary of the Cape Peninsula and is flanked in the north-west by Lions Head and Signal Hill, and in the northeast by Devil's Peak. The mountain slope linking Devil's Peak and Table Mountain is known as **'The Saddle'**. At the southern tip of the mountain lies **Orange Kloof**, whilst on its western slopes the famous **'Twelve Apostles'** tower high above the Atlantic Ocean.

The flat summit plateau overlooks the city and its highest point, at the eastern edge of the mountain, is **Maclear's Beacon** (1086 m). This beacon, a few years ago re-shaped into a conical cairn, was erected in 1844 by the Astronomer Royal, Sir Thomas Maclear, on a spot visible from the Observatory, Cape Point and Robben Island.

The original cable car station, designed by the Norwegian engineer T. Strömsee, was completed in 1929. The cable car was modernised in 1997. The rotating cabins transport 65 passengers a a time.

From a height of 1086 metres Table Mountain gradually slopes down in a southerly direction and the so-called Lower Table can easily be reached via the Bridle Path starting from Constantia Nek. Almost the entire mountain is ringed by contour paths: from Constantia Nek easy forest paths lead to Kirstenbosch National Botanical Gardens, from here a contour path leads on to the lower slopes of Devil's Peak from where it continues as a tarred road,

Tafelberg Road, to the lower cable car station , and then becomes, once again, a sand track winding around Kloof Corner and clinging to the lower slopes of the 'Twelve Apostles' - this stretch is known as the Pipe Track. The total distance of this network of paths is about 45 kilometres, almost two thirds of the mountain's circumference.

AN HISTORICAL OUTLINE TO 1806

For centuries Africa lived in peoples' minds as the dark, mysterious continent. Then came the Portuguese, their voyages of discovery, the first rounding of the Cape, and slowly the mystery unravelled. Few people realise, however, that Africa had already been circumnavigated in the 7th century B.C. The bold Pharaoh Necho dispatched three ships which commenced their adventurous journey by clinging to the east coast. After months, possibly years of hardships and deprivations the brave Phoenicians finally entered the Straits of Gibraltar. The voyage was documented by the Greek historian Herodotus, but the new-found knowledge gained by the Phoenicians remained locked away until the Portuguese set foot on African soil. This was in 1488 when Dias became the first modern navigator to circumnavigate the Cape of Good Hope.

His journey ended in present day Port Elizabeth where his mutinous crew forced him to return home. **Vasco da Gama** finally established the lucrative maritime route to the East in 1497.

The Cape that you have discovered was inhabited by the pastoralist **Khoikhoi** and the nomadic **San**, also known as Bushmen, when the Europeans landed. Khoikhoi means 'Men of Men', and San, the 'Gatherer'. The pastoralist **Khoikoi** excelled in many crafts, such as curing animal skins for clothing, bags and blankets. They shaped pottery and from shells,copper,ivory and later brass, they crafted attractive ornaments, particularly anklets and armlets.

The Khoikhoi lived in groups under a chief. As each group owned its own pasture land inter group cattle raiding occurred frequently. Pasture and water rights were strictly controlled. It was probably the Portuguese' lack of understanding of these fundamental rights that led to early clashes between the Khoi and the Europeans.

When the Dutch settled at the Cape in 1652, the Khoikhoi's cattle herds decreased rapidly. It is questionable whether or not a fair price in copper or tobacco was paid in return for livestock. Diminishing herds led to diminishing land tenure and as they lost their pasture land to the white man, the Khoikhoi were ultimately forced into an existence of dependency on the European.

Their situation worsened when a smallpox epidemic claimed countless lives amongst the Khoikhoi in the early 18th century. Later, in the nineteenth century, mission stations were established for the Khoikhoi in Namaqualand, giving them some security of tenure.

The 'hunter gatherers', the **Bushman**, fared little better.

In small groups they roamed the countryside. Caves and rock overhangs sheltered them from harsh weather. Their graceful rock paintings reflect their life and the world surrounding them. Cheerful and merry, the San loved dancing and music. Their survival depended on availability of water, game and their own hunting skills.

To the San, the desert, veld and mountains signified home, a gift from 'Naua', or Fate. His belief that all game belonged to him resulted in fierce retaliation against all those who poached on his possessions. But above all else, the San protected his watering-places.

Defenceless against the superior power of the Europeans' rifles, the San resorted to cattle theft which brought the full wrath of the whites upon him. He was hunted, enslaved and killed. In the late 18th century, horrific punitive raids were organised against them. The survivors sought refuge in the dry desert of the hinterland. His fate intermingled increasingly with that of the other races and today only few pure blooded San survive.

Let us return to the year 1497 which had established the maritime route to the east and ushered in an era of discoveries, expeditions and exploits. Shipping around the Cape increased considerably despite the hardships suffered by men and ships alike.

One well known early visitor was Sir Francis Drake. His 'Golden Hind' rounded the Cape in 1581, which he described as 'the most stately thing, and the fairest Cape in the whole circumference of the earth'. Yet the cloak of the unknown, mysterious still lay heavily over the Cape. The most vital life line, fresh water, had not yet been discovered.

Years after the 'Golden Hind' another English fleet dropped anchor in Table Bay. The dangerously low water supply on board forced the sailors to reconnoitre the shore. Fortunately for them, they chanced upon a stream. The discovery of seemingly abundant fresh water was to change the fate of the Cape. It was to lead towards the establishment of a provision station, a settlement, something which would greatly favour trade with the East Indies. England appeared reluctant to act on this thrilling discovery, other than landing some convicts on the shores of the Cape of Good Hope.

This first, pitiful attempt at settlement ended almost predictably, in disaster. Over a century would pass before Britain gained a firm foothold at the southern tip of Africa.

Countless adventurers, traders and whalers from Portugal, Holland and England came, but none settled at the wild and inhospitable coast. Only when the maritime power of the Portuguese had been broken and Holland stepped into the leadership rôle, was the Cape to awaken from its Cinderella sleep.

Within a year of independence from Spain in the late 16th century, Dutch ships were plying the oceans en route to the East. They anchored off Saldanha Bay -today's Table Bay- named after the Portuguese **Admiral Antonio de Saldanha** who had ascended Table Mountain in 1502 to establish his bearings; almost one hundred years later, in 1601, the Dutch seafarer, Joris van Spilbergen, re-named it Table Bay.

In the Netherlands, small trading companies amalgamated and formed the **Dutch East India Company**, also known as the **V.O.C** 'Vereenigde Oostindiese Companjie'.

The government invested the Company with far reaching powers in its founding charter. In time, these powers went far beyond that of regulating trade: it could i.a.enter into treaties, appoint legal personnel and call up an army. It was given control over a vast area, from the Cape to the Straits of Magellan. In the east, Djakarta in Indonesia, as from 1621 also known as **Batavia**, became the administrative capital.

The Company enjoyed phenomenal growth. In less than two decades its vessels had reached distant lands such as Siam, Japan, Java, Timor, Australia, the Fiji Islands, Mauritius, Ceylon (Sri Lanka) and China.

In 1649, one of her ships, the 'Nieeuw Haerlem' became a victim of a merciless storm in Table Bay, though captain and crew made it to the safety of the shore. Waiting for a rescue vessel, they gathered valuable information on explorative outings. Once delivered from their ordeal, the captain submitted the findings to the Company's Directors. This report which fell on receptive ears, recommended the establishment of a refreshment station at the Cape in favour of St. Helena which had served the Dutch since the early 1640's as a port.

The Company selected Jan van Riebeeck, an energetic merchant and ship's surgeon, for this pioneering task. Accompanied by his wife Marie de la

Queillerie and his young son, he sailed forth in 'Dromedaris'. His ship and the escorting fleet consisting of the 'Goede Hoop', 'Olifant' and 'Reijger', reached the Cape after a hundred and four days. Anchors were cast on 6 April 1652.

The rule of the Dutch East India Company at the Cape saw a rapid expansion of the borders, particularly eastward, placing enormous stress on the authorities to keep law and order. But more importantly, expansion, strife and corruption severely tested the financial resources. These were exhausted by the end of the 18th century. The economic gloom was temporarily brightened with the 3-year sojourn of French troops in Cape Town from 1781 to 1784. This friendly occupation came to pass as a direct result of the American War of Independence. This war, unleashed by England's colonies on the North American east coast, pitted England against Holland and France. French ships, as allies of the Dutch, landed at the Cape breathing a little French gaiety into the otherwise staid colony. Cape Town blossomed into a 'Little Paris'; merchants, shopkeepers, farmers filled their coffers. But the Company's woes increased as it was responsible for the upkeep of the forces. When the French finally left in 1784, Europe had embarked on a path prepared by philosophers and writers such as Jean Jacques Rousseau that was to lead to the outbreak of the French Revolution in 1789. Once again, the Cape's history mirrored events in Europe. The revolutionary spirit spread swiftly. Amsterdam fell to the French whilst the Prince of Orange fled to England seeking asylum and assistance. Willing to accede to the Prince's request to temporarily protect the Cape, England dispatched a powerful fleet. This intervention ended with the First British Occupation of the Cape in 1795. Barely eight years later, the Dutch once more regained their foothold. Yet this brief Batavian interlude ended in 1806 with the Second British Occupation. The Cape capitulated and the **PEACE TREATY OF PARIS**, 1814, ceded the territory to the English.

OTHER STORIES TOLD

WHY THE DASSIE HAS NO TAIL

As you watched the dassie lazying in the sunshine, did you wonder why it had no tail? A delightful Xhosa story tells us why.

A long time ago, long before man was even created, the lion was king of all animals. A most distinguished king he was too, as he alone possessed a tail. Sure, he was very proud of his tail and liked to parade before his subjects. But there were moments when he felt sorry for the other animals, as he had realised that a tail was not only something beautiful to possess but also very useful. Sometimes he even felt the odd one out, sensing the other animals' stare, their jealousy. Thus Lion, the King, decided one fine day that he would make tails for all his subjects and present them personally. How his eyes glowed in anticipation! What a wonderful surprise it would be!

Busily he set to work crafting tails in all sorts of wondrous shapes and sizes. When it was accomplished, he contentedly looked at his work. Then he summoned Baboon ordering him to call all animals to appear before him.

Far and wide Baboon ran and passed on the royal order. Hurriedly the animals set off to the Lion's court and by nightfall all had arrived, except Dassie. Dassie had begged Baboon to collect his present for him and to let the King know that he felt far too ashamed to appear before him. Being good-natured, Baboon had agreed.

The King warmly greeted his subjects standing expectantly around him and began to hand out the presents. Despite the bright moon the ageing King with his fading eyesight could not always distinguish the size and shape of tail he pulled out of a great sack. Thus, as mighty Elephant stood expectantly before him, the King passed a thin, curly little tail to this giant. Of course, Elephant was far too polite to protest and trotted off. When it was squirrel's turn, the King handed him a big bushy tail, far too big for such a little animal. But like Elephant, Squirrel hopped off gratefully. The sack emptied. Suddenly Lion noticed that Dassie was missing and roared at Baboon who in all the excitement had forgotten to pass on Dassie's apology. The King was furious but in the end agreed to let Baboon take the present to Dassie.

He picked a long tail for Dassie. As the festivities drew to an end, Baboon set off to bring Dassie his present. The road was long, the day had been long and Baoon was exhausted. He rested on a rocky ledge. Suddenly he jumped up, picked up the tail meant for Dassie and tied it to his own! 'Dassie does not deserve a present. Lazy fellow that he is.' Nonetheless, he wanted to teach Dassie a lesson. He sauntered off to Dassie's rocky home and showed off his lovely tail, mocking poor little Dassie. Of course, Dassie was upset that he would have no tail, but far too lazy to do anything about it.

WHY THE OSTRICH IS SO DUMB

An amusing bushman/San story reveals why the ostrich is so dumb.

Mantis, the Creator had accomplished his wonderful task, all animals had been created. He was pleased with his work and cast one last glance over the assembled animals before returning to Heaven. Suddenly his gaze fell upon the very sad looking ostrich. 'What have I done?' 'A big, wonderful bird, but I forgot to teach him how to fly!' Mantis felt terribly upset and desperately sought a way to make amends. 'Ah', he said, 'There is one thing I can ask ostrich to do for me. Him alone I can trust.' Mantis had until now hesitated to release the fire he had created as he feared that whoever possessed it, would destroy himself with it. Mantis approached the ostrich and asked him whether he would guard the fire for him? The ostrich felt extremely honoured to have been selected for such an important task and promised that he would secure the fire under one of his wings until the Creator would order him to release it. Feeling reassured, Mantis now took leave of the animals and returned to Heaven.

The ostrich, day after day, stood proudly in the fields mindful of his promise. Then Mantis created the first bushman who was very quick to discover ostrich's secret and knew what he was keeping under his wings. Desperately the bushman thought of ways to wrest the fire from the ostrich. Fire would keep him warm in the cold desert nights, with fire he could cook a meal! One morning, the bushman who could talk to the animals, approached the ostrich.

'Oh, ostrich, I have had such a wonderful dream; I have such good news for you!' The ostrich, curious, turned around wanting to find out more about the dream. 'I dreamed', said the bushman, 'that you could fly!'. Now he truly had the bird's attention. 'How did I fly? How did I do it'? Craftily the bushman told him that in his dream he had seen ostrich walk up a hill at dawn. On the crest of the hill he had closed his eyes, opened his wings whilst he kept his eyes closed all the time, and had soared into the air.' The ostrich was most intrigued. He managed to conceal his excitement from the bushman for a few days. But then, one morning believing to be the first awake, the ostrich stalked up the hill, paused a moment, never noticing that the bushman had followed him. Then the ostrich closed his eyes, spread his wings and, before he realised what was happening, the bushman had snatched the fire away from him, running as fast as could down the hill. Poor ostrich was so disturbed and upset by what he had done, that he lost his senses and became quite feeble minded.

VAN HUNK AND THE DEVIL

One day, Van Hunk, a retired pirate, sat as usual on the mountain slope linking Table Mountain with the 'Windberg', smoking peacefully his pipe. He savoured these moments, getting away from his constantly nagging wife who would not allow him to smoke in the home. Van Hunk looked down on the town stretched out below him. Then there were footsteps; he turned around and a very strangely clad man stood before him. Van Hunk beckoned him to sit down next to him. The stranger limped closer, he walked as if his boots were pinching him, a couple of sizes too small; a long, black cape was draped around his shoulders. Silently he sat down. No words were spoken, an uneasy feeling gripped Van Hunk. Somehow the stranger reminded him of his long forgotten pirate's days... Then suddenly, the stranger called him by his name, asking for a puff.. perplexed, Van Hunk passed the stranger some of his tobacco, boasting at the same time that nobody could smoke as long or as much as he could. The mysterious stranger replied: "I bet I am better than you." "What is the stake?" "Your soul" replied the stranger, "if I win", "a gold coin, if you win". Van Hunk gleefully accepted the bet, utterly confident that soon the gold coin would be his. They lit the pipes. The town below bathed in the golden afternoon sun. The hours passed. Silence... thicker and thicker rose the smoke, enveloping the men, night began to fall and still they smoked. Next morning a huge cloud hid the mountain, and a strong wind was gusting up. The stranger suddenly paled, then turned green and blue and finally collapsed."I'am burning", he moaned," give me something to drink!"

Unable to bear the heat any longer, the stranger ripped off his hood and bared two horns ! Now the cape came off, the devil stood before him. Van Hunk's terror knew no end; he scarcely heard the devil shouting at him that he would not pay him the gold coin...thunder and lightning erupted, a red cloud gathered. By the time Van Hunk recovered from his shock, the cloud had gone, the devil had disappeared - he ran down the mountain which ever since then was called "Devil's Peak", the mountain where he nearly lost his soul to the devil.

Devil's Peak, Table Mountain and Lion's Head

A BRIEF STATISTICAL PROFILE

(extracts from the 'Cape of Good Hope Business Guide' published by the Cape Chamber of Commerce, 1999)

The Cape Peninsula forms the southern tip of the Western Cape, the fourth largest province of the country's nine provinces, measuring about 129370 km². The Peninsula is bounded by the Hottentot Holland Mountains, Atlantic seaboard and the False Bay coastline. Although it is small - it covers a mere 4% of South Africa's total land area, it boasts nearly 10% of the country's arable soils. Despite the lack of mineral resources in the Western Cape as a whole,-the nearest mining developments are more than 300 km away from Cape Town-, the region is nonetheless a major export channel for minerals extracted in the north-western and north-eastern part of the Western Cape.

The population of the Western Cape numbers currently about 4,2 million, representing a very diverse society of many cultures, races and religions. More than half of the population (about 55%) is Coloured, 1% Asian, followed in almost equal percentages by the white/black population groups (about 20 % each).

The annual population growth is estimated to be 2,5% and scarcely 13% of the population can be considered as rural. The drift to the city and towns continues unabated, leading to the establishment of vast informal settlements. Close to 65% of the Province's people live in the Cape Metropolitan area, and a staggering 85% of the Province's gross regional product is produced in the metropole.

The diversity of cultures finds expression in a similar diversity of languages: about 59% consider Afrikaans as their home language, 20% English, a mere 0,7% speak both English and Afrikaans at home, whereas 19% of the population speak Xhosa and the remainder a variety of languages, including Zulu, Sesotho, Chinese and Gujarati.

About 67% of the labour force of approximately 1,8 million people finds employment in the formal sector, and 14,5% are engaged in informal activities; the rest is either unemployed or engaged in what can be referred to as survival activities, such as the street vendors. Unemployment overall in the Western Cape stands at 18,2 % of the labour force.

The social, personal and government services sectors provide about 16,1% of employment, followed by the manufacturing and mining sector with 14,4%, commerce, catering and accommodation sectors with 8,4% agriculture, forestry and fishing 9,1%, construction and repairs 7,5% and financial and business services 5,8%.

BIBLIOGRAPHY

The Historical Monuments
Of South Africa by J.J. Oberholster

The Rembrandt van Rijn
Foundation For Culture, 1972

Under Lion's Head by M. Murray

A.A. Balkema Cape Town 1964

An Illustrated Dictionary Of
South African History

Ibis Books and Editorial Services cc, 1994

The Cape Malays by I.D.du Plessis

A.A.Balkema Cape Town 1992

Bay Between the Mountains
by Arderne Tredgold

Human & Rousseau Cape Town,
Pretoria 1985

Life at the Cape a Hundred Years Ago
by a Lady

C. Struik Cape Town 1963

Between Two Shores
by M. Fraser and L.McMahon

David Philip Cape Town, Johannesburg, 1994

Plant Invaders

Cape Department of Nature and
Environmental Conservation, 1978

The Great South African Outdoors

Readers' Digest Association of South Africa
(Pty) Ltd Cape Town 1992

Wild Flowers of Table Mountain
by W.P.U. Jackson

Howard Timmins Cape Town 1977

Robben Island: The Politics Of Rock And Sand
by N.Penn, H.Deacon, N.Alexander

Department of Adult Education & Extra
Mural Studies, University of Cape Town, 1992

Whale Watching in South Africa
The Southern Right Whale
by Peter B. Best

Mammal Research Institute
University of Pretoria 1995

Mammals of the National Parks

Struik Publishers (Pty)Ltd 1995

The Ostrich
Anita Holtzhausen, Marlene Kotze

C.P. Nel Museum Oudtshoorn

Birds of Southern Africa by Kenneth Newman

Southern Book Publishers 1988

Sea Point Contact — Site C

Geological Society of South Africa

Groot Constantia
by Hans Fransen

SA Cultural History Museum
Cape Town 1983

Discovering Southern Africa
By T.V. Bulpin

Discovering Southern Africa Productions cc 1992

A BRIEF INDEX

A

Adamastor	59
Admiralty	76
Aerial Ropeway	76
African Black Oystercatche	46
African Penguin	64
Afrikander, H.M.S.	72
Agulhas	56
American War of Independence	67
Amiens, treaty of	69
African National Congress	87
Anreith, Anton	81,89
Antipolis	25
Assyrian Kings	40
Athens	15
Autshumao	25

B

Baboons	9,52
Baird, General	70
Baker, Sir Herbert	95
Bantry Bay	18
Basson, Willem	28
Batavia	102
Bellows	50
Bellsfontein Kramat	23
Benguela	56
Black Rocks	45
Blockhouses	97
Bontebok	61
Boomslang Cave	82
Bordjiesdrif	45
Botany Bay	18
Boulder's Beach	64
Boyes Drive	80
British Hotel	73
Brydegroom	10
Buffel's Bay	45
Buses and trams	20
Bushman	101

C

Cabo Tormentoso	58
Caledon, Lord	22
Camissa	10
Camps Bay	18,21,22

Cape Agulhas	56
Cape Doctor	19
Cape Floral Kingdom	43
Cape Fur Seal	26
Cape Glass Comp.	78
Cape of Good Hope	42,43,47,52
Cape of Storms	8
Cape Point	34,49,52,53,54,56
Cape Point Ostrich farm	40
Caravelle	59
Cassowary	40
Castle	13,30
Chacma baboon	52
Chapman, John	31
Chapman's Peak	31
Chapman's Peak Drive	8,28,30
Clan Monroe	37,38
Clarke, General	69
Clifton	21
Clovelly	80
Cloete family	89
Connaught, prince	28,71
Consent	31
Constantia, Klein	90
Constantiaberg	30
Cook, Captain	17,59
Cormorant	46,51
Craig, General	30,68
Cuvier, Baron	52

D

Da Gama, Vasco	13,45,47,60
Danger Point	33
Darwin, Charles	17
Dassies	49
De Camoes	59
De Lille	69
De Pass, Aaron	89
De Saldanha	102
De Waal	28
Devil's Peak	96
Dias	13,45,46,51,58,60
Die Boer	42
Disa	27
Dockyard Church	74
Drake, Sir Francis	101

Duncan Dock 11
Dutch Reformed Church 71

E
East Fort 30
Egyptian geese 46
Elphinstone, Adm. 68
Elsies Peak 78
Emu 40
Erica 43

F
First British Occupation 69
Fish Hoek 79
FitzHerbert 18
Floristic Kingdoms 44
Flying Dutchman 60
Fort Djanet 40
Fort Wyngard 11
Fynbos 43,44

G
Geldkis 22
Geological contact 16
George III 13
George V 60
Gifkommetjie 45
Glencairn 78
Golden Acre 10
Goringhaiquas 21
Green Point 15
Green Point Lighthouse 12
Grey, Sir George 11
Groot Constantia 88
Gurney, Walter 28

H
Hangklip, Cape 55
Henneman, Bishop 35
Hospital Terrace 72
Hout Bay 25,26
Hout Bay Museum 28

I
Imhoff 13,34
Indian Ocean 55
Isselsteijn 66

J
John, king 58

Johnstone, Commander 67
Jubilee Square 72
Judas Peak 42
Just Nuisance 72

K
Kakapo 32,33
Kalk Bay 80,81
Kamp, Fritz von 22
Katzenellenbogen 16
Kelp 50
Khoikhoi 21,25,100
Kingsley, Mary 74
Kipling, Rudyard 95
Kirstenbosch 92,93,94
Kiwi 40
Kronendal 26,27,28

L
Labia, Natale 85
Lancaster, Sir J. 13
Le Vaillant 55
Leopard 28
Liesching, Ludwig 18,19
Lighthouse 54
Lion's Head 16,18
Little Paris 67
Llundudno 25
Lobster 50
Lusitania 50,51

M
Maclear 54,93
Maiden's Cove 21
Mandela 86
Manganese Mining 29
Mariner's Wharf 26
Martello Tower 70
Masey, F. 95
Miller's Point 63
Mitfrod-Barberton 28
Mostert Mill 96
Mouille Point 11,12
Muizenberg 69,82,85
Muslim 24

N
Naval Museum 74
Nefertar, Queen 40
Nelson, Lord 69,76

Noon Gun	13,15	Smiswinkel Bay	63
Norbetines	36	Snoek	81
Nureelmobeen	23	Somerset Hospital	11
		Somerset, Lord	22,79
O		South Easter	19
Ocean View	34,39	Southern Right Whale	63
Old Residency	75	St. Francis	75
Olifantsbos	44	St. Peter	28
Ostrich	40	St. Pierre	67
Ou Kaapse Weg	34	St.James	82
Oude Kraal	25	St.Simon&St.Jude	71
		Stempastorie	71
P		Steppe Buzzard	90
Palace Barracks	76	Strandlopers	25
Pannekoek	22		
Papendorf	70	**T**	
Paris, Peace of	70	Thibault, Louis	87,89
Paulsberg	42	Thomas T.Tucker	44
Penguins	64	Three Anchor Bay	16
Perlemoen	47	Time Balls	15
Platboom	46	Titans	59
Pondicherry	31	Tokai Manor House	87
Popham, Sir	70	Twelve Apostles	21,22,98
Posthuys	84	Two Oceans Marathon	8
Prince of Orange	68		
Peers Cave	79	**U**	
		Umhlali	38
R			
Red Disa	27	**V**	
Renosterveld	44	Van der Decken	60
Restio	43	Van der Stel, Simon	66,76,88,90,91
Rhea	40	Van Riebeeck	21,26,28,93
Rhodes	83,84,94	Vasco da Gama	45,47,60
Robben Island	11,13,14,23	Venus Pools	45
Roman Rock Lighthouse	78	Visser,Antoni	66,70
Rooihoogte	42		
Rooikrans	47	**W**	
Rubbi	34,35	Watts, G.F.	95
		Warrior Toy Museum	72
S		Whales	63
San	40,100,101	Witsand	39
Scarborough	39	World of Birds	27
Schutte, Hermann	12,74		
Sea Fisheries	17,27	**Y**	
Sea Point	16,17,20	Yellowtail	47
Seafarer	15		
Signal Hill	13,16,18	**Z**	
Simon's Town	66,70	Zebra	61
Skaife, S.	45	Zeus	59
Slangkop Lighthouse	37,39	Ziegler, de	18,19